Mometrix
TEST PREPARATION

Common Core Grade 12 English Language Arts Secrets Study Guide

I0894331

DEAR FUTURE EXAM SUCCESS STORY

First of all, **THANK YOU** for purchasing Mometrix study materials!

Second, congratulations! You are one of the few determined test-takers who are committed to doing whatever it takes to excel on your exam. **You have come to the right place.** We developed these study materials with one goal in mind: to deliver you the information you need in a format that's concise and easy to use.

In addition to optimizing your guide for the content of the test, we've outlined our recommended steps for breaking down the preparation process into small, attainable goals so you can make sure you stay on track.

We've also analyzed the entire test-taking process, identifying the most common pitfalls and showing how you can overcome them and be ready for any curveball the test throws you.

Standardized testing is one of the biggest obstacles on your road to success, which only increases the importance of doing well in the high-pressure, high-stakes environment of test day. Your results on this test could have a significant impact on your future, and this guide provides the information and practical advice to help you achieve your full potential on test day.

Your success is our success

We would love to hear from you! If you would like to share the story of your exam success or if you have any questions or comments in regard to our products, please contact us at **800-673-8175** or **support@mometrix.com**.

Thanks again for your business and we wish you continued success!

Sincerely,
The Mometrix Test Preparation Team

Need more help? Check out our flashcards at:
http://MometrixFlashcards.com/CCSS

Written and edited by the Mometrix Exam Secrets Test Prep Team
Printed in the United States of America

TABLE OF CONTENTS

Introduction

Thank you for purchasing this resource! You have made the choice to prepare yourself for a test that could have a huge impact on your future, and this guide is designed to help you be fully ready for test day. Obviously, it's important to have a solid understanding of the test material, but you also need to be prepared for the unique environment and stressors of the test, so that you can perform to the best of your abilities.

For this purpose, the first section that appears in this guide is the **Secret Keys**. We've devoted countless hours to meticulously researching what works and what doesn't, and we've boiled down our findings to the five most impactful steps you can take to improve your performance on the test. We start at the beginning with study planning and move through the preparation process, all the way to the testing strategies that will help you get the most out of what you know when you're finally sitting in front of the test.

We recommend that you start preparing for your test as far in advance as possible. However, if you've bought this guide as a last-minute study resource and only have a few days before your test, we recommend that you skip over the first two Secret Keys since they address a long-term study plan.

If you struggle with **test anxiety**, we strongly encourage you to check out our recommendations for how you can overcome it. Test anxiety is a formidable foe, but it can be beaten, and we want to make sure you have the tools you need to defeat it.

Secret Key #1 – Plan Big, Study Small

There's a lot riding on your performance. If you want to ace this test, you're going to need to keep your skills sharp and the material fresh in your mind. You need a plan that lets you review everything you need to know while still fitting in your schedule. We'll break this strategy down into three categories.

Information Organization

Start with the information you already have: the official test outline. From this, you can make a complete list of all the concepts you need to cover before the test. Organize these concepts into groups that can be studied together, and create a list of any related vocabulary you need to learn so you can brush up on any difficult terms. You'll want to keep this vocabulary list handy once you actually start studying since you may need to add to it along the way.

Time Management

Once you have your set of study concepts, decide how to spread them out over the time you have left before the test. Break your study plan into small, clear goals so you have a manageable task for each day and know exactly what you're doing. Then just focus on one small step at a time. When you manage your time this way, you don't need to spend hours at a time studying. Studying a small block of content for a short period each day helps you retain information better and avoid stressing over how much you have left to do. You can relax knowing that you have a plan to cover everything in time. In order for this strategy to be effective though, you have to start studying early and stick to your schedule. Avoid the exhaustion and futility that comes from last-minute cramming!

Study Environment

The environment you study in has a big impact on your learning. Studying in a coffee shop, while probably more enjoyable, is not likely to be as fruitful as studying in a quiet room. It's important to keep distractions to a minimum. You're only planning to study for a short block of time, so make the most of it. Don't pause to check your phone or get up to find a snack. It's also important to **avoid multitasking**. Research has consistently shown that multitasking will make your studying dramatically less effective. Your study area should also be comfortable and well-lit so you don't have the distraction of straining your eyes or sitting on an uncomfortable chair.

The time of day you study is also important. You want to be rested and alert. Don't wait until just before bedtime. Study when you'll be most likely to comprehend and remember. Even better, if you know what time of day your test will be, set that time aside for study. That way your brain will be used to working on that subject at that specific time and you'll have a better chance of recalling information.

Finally, it can be helpful to team up with others who are studying for the same test. Your actual studying should be done in as isolated an environment as possible, but the work of organizing the information and setting up the study plan can be divided up. In between study sessions, you can discuss with your teammates the concepts that you're all studying and quiz each other on the details. Just be sure that your teammates are as serious about the test as you are. If you find that your study time is being replaced with social time, you might need to find a new team.

Secret Key #2 – Make Your Studying Count

You're devoting a lot of time and effort to preparing for this test, so you want to be absolutely certain it will pay off. This means doing more than just reading the content and hoping you can remember it on test day. It's important to make every minute of study count. There are two main areas you can focus on to make your studying count.

Retention

It doesn't matter how much time you study if you can't remember the material. You need to make sure you are retaining the concepts. To check your retention of the information you're learning, try recalling it at later times with minimal prompting. Try carrying around flashcards and glance at one or two from time to time or ask a friend who's also studying for the test to quiz you.

To enhance your retention, look for ways to put the information into practice so that you can apply it rather than simply recalling it. If you're using the information in practical ways, it will be much easier to remember. Similarly, it helps to solidify a concept in your mind if you're not only reading it to yourself but also explaining it to someone else. Ask a friend to let you teach them about a concept you're a little shaky on (or speak aloud to an imaginary audience if necessary). As you try to summarize, define, give examples, and answer your friend's questions, you'll understand the concepts better and they will stay with you longer. Finally, step back for a big picture view and ask yourself how each piece of information fits with the whole subject. When you link the different concepts together and see them working together as a whole, it's easier to remember the individual components.

Finally, practice showing your work on any multi-step problems, even if you're just studying. Writing out each step you take to solve a problem will help solidify the process in your mind, and you'll be more likely to remember it during the test.

Modality

Modality simply refers to the means or method by which you study. Choosing a study modality that fits your own individual learning style is crucial. No two people learn best in exactly the same way, so it's important to know your strengths and use them to your advantage.

For example, if you learn best by visualization, focus on visualizing a concept in your mind and draw an image or a diagram. Try color-coding your notes, illustrating them, or creating symbols that will trigger your mind to recall a learned concept. If you learn best by hearing or discussing information, find a study partner who learns the same way or read aloud to yourself. Think about how to put the information in your own words. Imagine that you are giving a lecture on the topic and record yourself so you can listen to it later.

For any learning style, flashcards can be helpful. Organize the information so you can take advantage of spare moments to review. Underline key words or phrases. Use different colors for different categories. Mnemonic devices (such as creating a short list in which every item starts with the same letter) can also help with retention. Find what works best for you and use it to store the information in your mind most effectively and easily.

Secret Key #3 – Practice the Right Way

Your success on test day depends not only on how many hours you put into preparing, but also on whether you prepared the right way. It's good to check along the way to see if your studying is paying off. One of the most effective ways to do this is by taking practice tests to evaluate your progress. Practice tests are useful because they show exactly where you need to improve. Every time you take a practice test, pay special attention to these three groups of questions:

- The questions you got wrong
- The questions you had to guess on, even if you guessed right
- The questions you found difficult or slow to work through

This will show you exactly what your weak areas are, and where you need to devote more study time. Ask yourself why each of these questions gave you trouble. Was it because you didn't understand the material? Was it because you didn't remember the vocabulary? Do you need more repetitions on this type of question to build speed and confidence? Dig into those questions and figure out how you can strengthen your weak areas as you go back to review the material.

Additionally, many practice tests have a section explaining the answer choices. It can be tempting to read the explanation and think that you now have a good understanding of the concept. However, an explanation likely only covers part of the question's broader context. Even if the explanation makes perfect sense, **go back and investigate** every concept related to the question until you're positive you have a thorough understanding.

As you go along, keep in mind that the practice test is just that: practice. Memorizing these questions and answers will not be very helpful on the actual test because it is unlikely to have any of the same exact questions. If you only know the right answers to the sample questions, you won't be prepared for the real thing. **Study the concepts** until you understand them fully, and then you'll be able to answer any question that shows up on the test.

It's important to wait on the practice tests until you're ready. If you take a test on your first day of study, you may be overwhelmed by the amount of material covered and how much you need to learn. Work up to it gradually.

On test day, you'll need to be prepared for answering questions, managing your time, and using the test-taking strategies you've learned. It's a lot to balance, like a mental marathon that will have a big impact on your future. Like training for a marathon, you'll need to start slowly and work your way up. When test day arrives, you'll be ready.

Start with the strategies you've read in the first two Secret Keys—plan your course and study in the way that works best for you. If you have time, consider using multiple study resources to get different approaches to the same concepts. It can be helpful to see difficult concepts from more than one angle. Then find a good source for practice tests. Many times, the test website will suggest potential study resources or provide sample tests.

Practice Test Strategy

If you're able to find at least three practice tests, we recommend this strategy:

Untimed and Open-Book Practice

Take the first test with no time constraints and with your notes and study guide handy. Take your time and focus on applying the strategies you've learned.

Timed and Open-Book Practice

Take the second practice test open-book as well, but set a timer and practice pacing yourself to finish in time.

Timed and Closed-Book Practice

Take any other practice tests as if it were test day. Set a timer and put away your study materials. Sit at a table or desk in a quiet room, imagine yourself at the testing center, and answer questions as quickly and accurately as possible.

Keep repeating timed and closed-book tests on a regular basis until you run out of practice tests or it's time for the actual test. Your mind will be ready for the schedule and stress of test day, and you'll be able to focus on recalling the material you've learned.

Secret Key #4 – Pace Yourself

Once you're fully prepared for the material on the test, your biggest challenge on test day will be managing your time. Just knowing that the clock is ticking can make you panic even if you have plenty of time left. Work on pacing yourself so you can build confidence against the time constraints of the exam. Pacing is a difficult skill to master, especially in a high-pressure environment, so **practice is vital**.

Set time expectations for your pace based on how much time is available. For example, if a section has 60 questions and the time limit is 30 minutes, you know you have to average 30 seconds or less per question in order to answer them all. Although 30 seconds is the hard limit, set 25 seconds per question as your goal, so you reserve extra time to spend on harder questions. When you budget extra time for the harder questions, you no longer have any reason to stress when those questions take longer to answer.

Don't let this time expectation distract you from working through the test at a calm, steady pace, but keep it in mind so you don't spend too much time on any one question. Recognize that taking extra time on one question you don't understand may keep you from answering two that you do understand later in the test. If your time limit for a question is up and you're still not sure of the answer, mark it and move on, and come back to it later if the time and the test format allow. If the testing format doesn't allow you to return to earlier questions, just make an educated guess; then put it out of your mind and move on.

On the easier questions, be careful not to rush. It may seem wise to hurry through them so you have more time for the challenging ones, but it's not worth missing one if you know the concept and just didn't take the time to read the question fully. Work efficiently but make sure you understand the question and have looked at all of the answer choices, since more than one may seem right at first.

Even if you're paying attention to the time, you may find yourself a little behind at some point. You should speed up to get back on track, but do so wisely. Don't panic; just take a few seconds less on each question until you're caught up. Don't guess without thinking, but do look through the answer choices and eliminate any you know are wrong. If you can get down to two choices, it is often worthwhile to guess from those. Once you've chosen an answer, move on and don't dwell on any that you skipped or had to hurry through. If a question was taking too long, chances are it was one of the harder ones, so you weren't as likely to get it right anyway.

On the other hand, if you find yourself getting ahead of schedule, it may be beneficial to slow down a little. The more quickly you work, the more likely you are to make a careless mistake that will affect your score. You've budgeted time for each question, so don't be afraid to spend that time. Practice an efficient but careful pace to get the most out of the time you have.

Secret Key #5 – Have a Plan for Guessing

When you're taking the test, you may find yourself stuck on a question. Some of the answer choices seem better than others, but you don't see the one answer choice that is obviously correct. What do you do?

The scenario described above is very common, yet most test takers have not effectively prepared for it. Developing and practicing a plan for guessing may be one of the single most effective uses of your time as you get ready for the exam.

In developing your plan for guessing, there are three questions to address:

- When should you start the guessing process?
- How should you narrow down the choices?
- Which answer should you choose?

When to Start the Guessing Process

Unless your plan for guessing is to select C every time (which, despite its merits, is not what we recommend), you need to leave yourself enough time to apply your answer elimination strategies. Since you have a limited amount of time for each question, that means that if you're going to give yourself the best shot at guessing correctly, you have to decide quickly whether or not you will guess.

Of course, the best-case scenario is that you don't have to guess at all, so first, see if you can answer the question based on your knowledge of the subject and basic reasoning skills. Focus on the key words in the question and try to jog your memory of related topics. Give yourself a chance to bring the knowledge to mind, but once you realize that you don't have (or you can't access) the knowledge you need to answer the question, it's time to start the guessing process.

It's almost always better to start the guessing process too early than too late. It only takes a few seconds to remember something and answer the question from knowledge. Carefully eliminating wrong answer choices takes longer. Plus, going through the process of eliminating answer choices can actually help jog your memory.

Summary: Start the guessing process as soon as you decide that you can't answer the question based on your knowledge.

How to Narrow Down the Choices

The next chapter in this book (**Test-Taking Strategies**) includes a wide range of strategies for how to approach questions and how to look for answer choices to eliminate. You will definitely want to read those carefully, practice them, and figure out which ones work best for you. Here though, we're going to address a mindset rather than a particular strategy.

Your odds of guessing an answer correctly depend on how many options you are choosing from.

Number of options left	5	4	3	2	1
Odds of guessing correctly	20%	25%	33%	50%	100%

You can see from this chart just how valuable it is to be able to eliminate incorrect answers and make an educated guess, but there are two things that many test takers do that cause them to miss out on the benefits of guessing:

- Accidentally eliminating the correct answer
- Selecting an answer based on an impression

We'll look at the first one here, and the second one in the next section.

To avoid accidentally eliminating the correct answer, we recommend a thought exercise called **the $5 challenge**. In this challenge, you only eliminate an answer choice from contention if you are willing to bet $5 on it being wrong. Why $5? Five dollars is a small but not insignificant amount of money. It's an amount you could afford to lose but wouldn't want to throw away. And while losing $5 once might not hurt too much, doing it twenty times will set you back $100. In the same way, each small decision you make—eliminating a choice here, guessing on a question there—won't by itself impact your score very much, but when you put them all together, they can make a big difference. By holding each answer choice elimination decision to a higher standard, you can reduce the risk of accidentally eliminating the correct answer.

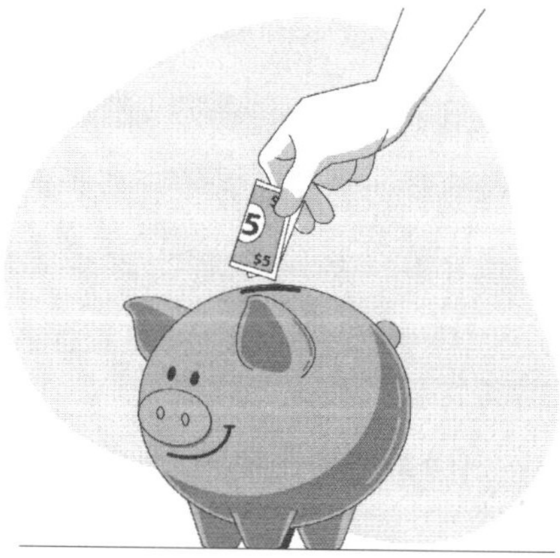

The $5 challenge can also be applied in a positive sense: If you are willing to bet $5 that an answer choice *is* correct, go ahead and mark it as correct.

Summary: Only eliminate an answer choice if you are willing to bet $5 that it is wrong.

Which Answer to Choose

You're taking the test. You've run into a hard question and decided you'll have to guess. You've eliminated all the answer choices you're willing to bet $5 on. Now you have to pick an answer. Why do we even need to talk about this? Why can't you just pick whichever one you feel like when the time comes?

The answer to these questions is that if you don't come into the test with a plan, you'll rely on your impression to select an answer choice, and if you do that, you risk falling into a trap. The test writers know that everyone who takes their test will be guessing on some of the questions, so they intentionally write wrong answer choices to seem plausible. You still have to pick an answer though, and if the wrong answer choices are designed to look right, how can you ever be sure that you're not falling for their trap? The best solution we've found to this dilemma is to take the decision out of your hands entirely. Here is the process we recommend:

Once you've eliminated any choices that you are confident (willing to bet $5) are wrong, select the first remaining choice as your answer.

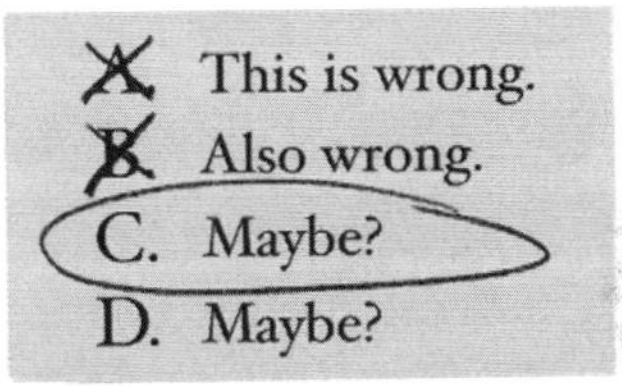

Whether you choose to select the first remaining choice, the second, or the last, the important thing is that you use some preselected standard. Using this approach guarantees that you will not be enticed into selecting an answer choice that looks right, because you are not basing your decision on how the answer choices look.

This is not meant to make you question your knowledge. Instead, it is to help you recognize the difference between your knowledge and your impressions. There's a huge difference between thinking an answer is right because of what you know, and thinking an answer is right because it looks or sounds like it should be right.

Summary: To ensure that your selection is appropriately random, make a predetermined selection from among all answer choices you have not eliminated.

Test-Taking Strategies

This section contains a list of test-taking strategies that you may find helpful as you work through the test. By taking what you know and applying logical thought, you can maximize your chances of answering any question correctly!

It is very important to realize that every question is different and every person is different: no single strategy will work on every question, and no single strategy will work for every person. That's why we've included all of them here, so you can try them out and determine which ones work best for different types of questions and which ones work best for you.

Question Strategies

✓ Read Carefully

Read the question and the answer choices carefully. Don't miss the question because you misread the terms. You have plenty of time to read each question thoroughly and make sure you understand what is being asked. Yet a happy medium must be attained, so don't waste too much time. You must read carefully and efficiently.

✓ Contextual Clues

Look for contextual clues. If the question includes a word you are not familiar with, look at the immediate context for some indication of what the word might mean. Contextual clues can often give you all the information you need to decipher the meaning of an unfamiliar word. Even if you can't determine the meaning, you may be able to narrow down the possibilities enough to make a solid guess at the answer to the question.

✓ Prefixes

If you're having trouble with a word in the question or answer choices, try dissecting it. Take advantage of every clue that the word might include. Prefixes can be a huge help. Usually, they allow you to determine a basic meaning. *Pre-* means before, *post-* means after, *pro-* is positive, *de-* is negative. From prefixes, you can get an idea of the general meaning of the word and try to put it into context.

✓ Hedge Words

Watch out for critical hedge words, such as *likely, may, can, often, almost, mostly, usually, generally, rarely,* and *sometimes.* Question writers insert these hedge phrases to cover every possibility. Often an answer choice will be wrong simply because it leaves no room for exception. Be on guard for answer choices that have definitive words such as *exactly* and *always.*

✓ Switchback Words

Stay alert for *switchbacks.* These are the words and phrases frequently used to alert you to shifts in thought. The most common switchback words are *but, although,* and *however.* Others include *nevertheless, on the other hand, even though, while, in spite of, despite,* and *regardless of.* Switchback words are important to catch because they can change the direction of the question or an answer choice.

✓ FACE VALUE

When in doubt, use common sense. Accept the situation in the problem at face value. Don't read too much into it. These problems will not require you to make wild assumptions. If you have to go beyond creativity and warp time or space in order to have an answer choice fit the question, then you should move on and consider the other answer choices. These are normal problems rooted in reality. The applicable relationship or explanation may not be readily apparent, but it is there for you to figure out. Use your common sense to interpret anything that isn't clear.

Answer Choice Strategies

✓ ANSWER SELECTION

The most thorough way to pick an answer choice is to identify and eliminate wrong answers until only one is left, then confirm it is the correct answer. Sometimes an answer choice may immediately seem right, but be careful. The test writers will usually put more than one reasonable answer choice on each question, so take a second to read all of them and make sure that the other choices are not equally obvious. As long as you have time left, it is better to read every answer choice than to pick the first one that looks right without checking the others.

✓ ANSWER CHOICE FAMILIES

An answer choice family consists of two (in rare cases, three) answer choices that are very similar in construction and cannot all be true at the same time. If you see two answer choices that are direct opposites or parallels, one of them is usually the correct answer. For instance, if one answer choice says that quantity *x* increases and another either says that quantity *x* decreases (opposite) or says that quantity *y* increases (parallel), then those answer choices would fall into the same family. An answer choice that doesn't match the construction of the answer choice family is more likely to be incorrect. Most questions will not have answer choice families, but when they do appear, you should be prepared to recognize them.

✓ ELIMINATE ANSWERS

Eliminate answer choices as soon as you realize they are wrong, but make sure you consider all possibilities. If you are eliminating answer choices and realize that the last one you are left with is also wrong, don't panic. Start over and consider each choice again. There may be something you missed the first time that you will realize on the second pass.

✓ AVOID FACT TRAPS

Don't be distracted by an answer choice that is factually true but doesn't answer the question. You are looking for the choice that answers the question. Stay focused on what the question is asking for so you don't accidentally pick an answer that is true but incorrect. Always go back to the question and make sure the answer choice you've selected actually answers the question and is not merely a true statement.

✓ EXTREME STATEMENTS

In general, you should avoid answers that put forth extreme actions as standard practice or proclaim controversial ideas as established fact. An answer choice that states the "process should be used in certain situations, if…" is much more likely to be correct than one that states the "process should be discontinued completely." The first is a calm rational statement and doesn't even make a definitive, uncompromising stance, using a hedge word *if* to provide wiggle room, whereas the second choice is far more extreme.

☑ BENCHMARK

As you read through the answer choices and you come across one that seems to answer the question well, mentally select that answer choice. This is not your final answer, but it's the one that will help you evaluate the other answer choices. The one that you selected is your benchmark or standard for judging each of the other answer choices. Every other answer choice must be compared to your benchmark. That choice is correct until proven otherwise by another answer choice beating it. If you find a better answer, then that one becomes your new benchmark. Once you've decided that no other choice answers the question as well as your benchmark, you have your final answer.

☑ PREDICT THE ANSWER

Before you even start looking at the answer choices, it is often best to try to predict the answer. When you come up with the answer on your own, it is easier to avoid distractions and traps because you will know exactly what to look for. The right answer choice is unlikely to be word-for-word what you came up with, but it should be a close match. Even if you are confident that you have the right answer, you should still take the time to read each option before moving on.

General Strategies

☑ TOUGH QUESTIONS

If you are stumped on a problem or it appears too hard or too difficult, don't waste time. Move on! Remember though, if you can quickly check for obviously incorrect answer choices, your chances of guessing correctly are greatly improved. Before you completely give up, at least try to knock out a couple of possible answers. Eliminate what you can and then guess at the remaining answer choices before moving on.

☑ CHECK YOUR WORK

Since you will probably not know every term listed and the answer to every question, it is important that you get credit for the ones that you do know. Don't miss any questions through careless mistakes. If at all possible, try to take a second to look back over your answer selection and make sure you've selected the correct answer choice and haven't made a costly careless mistake (such as marking an answer choice that you didn't mean to mark). This quick double check should more than pay for itself in caught mistakes for the time it costs.

☑ PACE YOURSELF

It's easy to be overwhelmed when you're looking at a page full of questions; your mind is confused and full of random thoughts, and the clock is ticking down faster than you would like. Calm down and maintain the pace that you have set for yourself. Especially as you get down to the last few minutes of the test, don't let the small numbers on the clock make you panic. As long as you are on track by monitoring your pace, you are guaranteed to have time for each question.

☑ DON'T RUSH

It is very easy to make errors when you are in a hurry. Maintaining a fast pace in answering questions is pointless if it makes you miss questions that you would have gotten right otherwise. Test writers like to include distracting information and wrong answers that seem right. Taking a little extra time to avoid careless mistakes can make all the difference in your test score. Find a pace that allows you to be confident in the answers that you select.

⊘ KEEP MOVING

Panicking will not help you pass the test, so do your best to stay calm and keep moving. Taking deep breaths and going through the answer elimination steps you practiced can help to break through a stress barrier and keep your pace.

Final Notes

The combination of a solid foundation of content knowledge and the confidence that comes from practicing your plan for applying that knowledge is the key to maximizing your performance on test day. As your foundation of content knowledge is built up and strengthened, you'll find that the strategies included in this chapter become more and more effective in helping you quickly sift through the distractions and traps of the test to isolate the correct answer.

Now that you're preparing to move forward into the test content chapters of this book, be sure to keep your goal in mind. As you read, think about how you will be able to apply this information on the test. If you've already seen sample questions for the test and you have an idea of the question format and style, try to come up with questions of your own that you can answer based on what you're reading. This will give you valuable practice applying your knowledge in the same ways you can expect to on test day.

Good luck and good studying!

Reading

Literature

Explicit Information

Explicit information includes facts and statements that are found directly in a passage or a story. It is not information that is hinted at or information you need to make a conclusion about. Explicit information may be found in many forms; it can be contained in a quote as well as in a description. It can be found in dialogue and in actions. This information can sometimes be used to support an inference. The answers to questions about explicit information are found through careful reading of the text. Attention is given to pertinent facts or other information. In fiction, details about characters, events, and setting can be both explicit and implicit.

Read the following excerpt and identify the information that is explicit.

> According to an ancient Greek legend, an inventor named Daedalus was imprisoned on an island by an angry king. His son, Icarus, was with him. The inventor came up with an escape plan. He created two pairs of wings from feathers and a wooden frame. He made one for himself and one for his son.

Explicit information is information found directly in the text. It is not inferred; it is not suggested. The explicit information in this excerpt is about the Greek myth that tells the story of the inventor Daedalus. The excerpt says that the inventor Daedalus and his son Icarus were imprisoned on an island by an angry king. It says that he had a plan of escape, and that he created two pairs of wings from feathers and a wooden frame. This information is found directly in the excerpt. It is not necessary to make any inferences or guesses to obtain this information.

Inference

An inference is a conclusion that a reader can make based on the facts and other information in a passage or a story. An inference is based both on what is found in a passage or a story and what is known from personal experience. For instance, a story may say that a character is frightened and that he can hear the sounds of wolves in the distance. Based on both what is in the text and personal knowledge, it might be a logical conclusion that the character is frightened because he hears the sound of wolves. A good inference is supported by the information in a passage. Inferences are different from explicit information, which is clearly stated in a passage. Inferences are not stated in a passage. A reader must put the information together to come up with a logical conclusion.

Read the excerpt and decide why Jana finally relaxed.

> Jana loved her job, but the work was very demanding. She had trouble relaxing. She called a friend, but she still thought about work. She ordered a pizza, but eating it did not help. Then her kitten jumped on her lap and began to purr. Jana leaned back and began to hum a little tune. She felt better.

You can draw the conclusion that Jana relaxes because her kitten jumped on her lap. The kitten purred, and Jana leaned back and hummed a tune. Then, she felt better. The excerpt does not explicitly say that this is the reason why she was able to relax. The text leaves the matter unclear. But, the reader can infer or make a "best guess" that this is the reason she is relaxing. This is a logical conclusion based on the information in the passage. It is the best conclusion a reader can make based on the information he or she has read. Inferences are based on the information in a passage, but they are not directly stated in the passage.

Determining the Theme of a Passage

The theme of a passage is what the reader learns from the text or the passage. It is the lesson or moral contained in the passage. A passage can have two or more themes that convey its overall idea. The theme or themes of a passage are often based on universal themes. They can frequently be expressed using well-known sayings about life, society, or human nature, such as "Hard work pays off" or "Good triumphs over evil." Themes are not usually stated explicitly. The reader must figure them out by carefully reading the passage. Themes are often the reason why passages are written; they give a passage unity and meaning. Themes are created through plot development. The events of a story help shape the themes of a passage.

Explain why "Take care of what you care about" accurately describes the theme of the following excerpt.

> Luca collected baseball cards. But, Luca wasn't very careful with them. He left them around the house. His dog liked to chew. Luca and his friend Bart were looking at his collection. Then, they went outside. When Luca got home, he saw his dog chewing on his cards. They were ruined.

This excerpt tells the story of a boy who is careless with his baseball cards and leaves them lying around. His dog ends up chewing them and ruining them. The lesson is that if you care about something, you need to take care of it. This is the point of the story. The theme is the lesson that a story teaches. Some stories have more than one theme, but this is not really true of this excerpt. The reader needs to figure out the theme based on what happens in the story. Sometimes, as in the case of fables, the theme is stated directly in the text. However, this is not usually the case.

Components of a Story Summary

A summary of a passage or a story should include the main ideas of a passage and also the important details that support the main ideas. It shouldn't just be a general statement about what a passage is about, but should include important events and other details that make the story what it is. In order to write an objective summary, you have to reflect on what the passage is about. A summary puts the information in a concise form. Consequently, summarizing is different from paraphrasing. Paraphrasing involves rewording the main idea and supporting ideas in a fairly detailed way; summarizing does not. Summaries afford the reader the opportunity to quickly review the main points of a passage and the important details.

Setting and Characters

Without characters and setting, there is no story. They affect the plot of a story in many ways. The setting creates the background for the action. The setting could be someplace exotic or mundane, but wherever it is, it creates limitations for the characters. Characters are also essential to a story. They bring the story to life; it is their decisions, what they do, and how they act that creates the plot of a story and ultimately its theme. Characters can have good traits and bad traits. Analyzing what these are based on what a character does and says is an important aspect of comprehending the meaning of a story.

Read the excerpt and explain how the setting influences the plot.

> The cave was dark, so dark that Ernesto could not see a thing. He could not see his hand in front of him. He was lost, and he knew that time was running out. He could hear the trickle of water somewhere in the distance. He knew he had to follow the sound. It was his only hope of escaping.

The setting of the cave creates a conflict since Ernesto cannot see a thing and is lost. The excerpt also says that Ernesto's time is running out. While the reader does not know why this is the case, this increases the tension in the story. The fact that Ernesto can hear the dripping of the water is also important to the plot, since it influences the events of the story. Ernesto decides he should go towards the sound of the water. Setting influences the plot here because it creates a struggle for the main character. It also influences the character since Ernesto makes choices about what he should do based on the setting.

Impact of the Order of a Story or Introduction of Characters Has on a Story

The way in which an author chooses to order the events of or introduce characters in a story has a strong effect on it. Most stories are told in chronological order; one event occurs after another. But, an author can influence the development of a story by placing one event out of order to emphasize its importance. Another technique used by some authors is a flashback, in which time changes from the present to the past. When it comes to introducing characters, authors have a great deal of latitude. Authors often introduce the most important characters first so that the reader will have time to get acquainted with the characters' past and present situations. Readers are often influenced by the author's feelings toward a particular character, which often have an effect on how a character is introduced.

Determining the Meaning of Words or Phrases as They Are Used in a Text

When the reader does not understand a word or a phrase that is used in a passage or a story, it is important to examine the context clues around the word or phrase that provide hints about its meaning. Many words have more than one meaning, and it is only through an examination of the context that the reader can figure out the correct meaning. The word "crown" is a good example. This word has several meanings, including a coronet, the top of a head, the act of awarding something to someone, or even the act of hitting someone. Therefore, it is important to understand the context. In the sentence, "He sought to be crowned the winner of the competition," it is clear that the meaning is "to be awarded." Context must also be used to determine the meaning of phrases. In the sentence, "He wasn't going to stand for that anymore, so he told his boss off," the reader can use context to get a sense of the meaning of "going to stand for." In this case, the phrase means "not put up with."

Figurative Use of a Word

Authors use literary devices like figurative language to expand reality in a vivid way. An author can utilize figurative language to connect things in an exaggerated way, which results in a stronger, more vivid image. Examples of figurative language include simile, metaphor, personification, and hyperbole. Similes compare things using the comparing words *like* or *as*. "She is as brave as a lion" is an example of a simile. Metaphors compare things without using comparing words. An example of a metaphor is "She is a lion in the wild." Personification attributes human traits to an animal or non-living thing. "Time flew by" is an example of personification. Hyperbole is an exaggeration that is not believable. "He waited in line for years" is an example of this literary device.

Read the excerpt; identify the form of figurative language represented by the phrase "like a fresh April shower," and explain your answer.

> We had been sequestered inside the barn all afternoon. It was hot, really hot. When the sun finally set and I opened the door, the evening air swept over us like a fresh April shower, leaving us ready to enjoy the evening.

The phrase "like a fresh April shower" is an example of a simile. The phrase compares the air with a fresh April shower and uses the word "like," so it qualifies as a simile. Similes compare two things using the word "like" or "as." This phrase is not a metaphor. Although it compares two things, it uses the word "like"; metaphors do not use either "like" or "as" to compare two things. It is not an example of personification, because nothing is being given human traits. There is no sign of hyperbole here either; there is no sense of an exaggeration.

Relationship Between the Denotative and Connotative Meaning of Words

The denotative meaning of a word and the connotative meaning are only alike in that, according to the dictionary, they mean the same thing. However, that is where the similarities end. The connotative meaning of a word is what is suggested above and beyond the literal meaning. For instance, the word "untidy" might mean "messy" or "unclean," whereas the word "slovenly" suggests something closer to "filthy." When writers create stories, they frequently use words that have strong connotations to describe and develop the characters and the setting. It is important for the reader to analyze these word choices to gain a better understanding of the author's purpose.

Read the following sentence.

I expected my gear to be inspected, but I never thought it would be scrutinized to this degree.

Explain the connotative meanings of the word "scrutinized" and how they relate to the word "inspected."

Both "scrutinized" and "inspected" have the dictionary meaning of being "closely looked at" or "studied." But, the word "scrutinized" means that something is being dissected and analyzed, not just inspected or checked out. The word "scrutinized" is a much stronger term than the word "inspected." Many things are inspected, but not everything is scrutinized. It is important to choose words that fit the situation, something that is done in this sentence. The connotations that a word brings to a sentence will impact the way a reader comprehends what is being written about. Words with strong connotations help a reader get a feel for what is being written about.

Impact of Words on Tone

Words can have a large impact on the tone of a passage. Tone is a result of the choice of language. For instance, when talking about or suggesting the mood of a person or a setting, it is vital to choose the right language to describe it. Is a person ecstatic, or is the person simply content? Is a room barren, or is it just empty? Similarly, using strong action verbs can create a tone that is forceful and remembered easily. The verb *buttress*, for instance, has a much stronger impact than the verb *strengthen*. Even though both words have basically the same meaning, the first one creates a more vivid image in the mind of the reader. It is important to use words that will be understood by the audience and will have the desired effect.

Fresh and Engaging Language

One way to get a reader's attention and hold it is to use language that is fresh and engaging. Using a personal point of view is a good way to accomplish this. You should try to generate excitement by using a different perspective. Always avoid clichés—they will come across as stale and worn out. Learning editing skills is useful; it will help you eliminate unnecessary portions of a text. Use a dictionary and a thesaurus to locate the words you are looking for, and analyze the words to determine how a reader might perceive them. Finally, read your passage aloud to see how it sounds.

Read the excerpt. Describe why the language is fresh and engaging.

"Full many a glorious morning have I seen
Flatter the mountain tops with sovereign eye,
Kissing with golden face the meadows green,
Gilding pale streams with heavenly alchemy;"
(Shakespeare, Sonnet XXXIII)

In these few lines, Shakespeare provides the reader with a fresh, new image of nature. Morning is personified as a romantic king in love with the meadows and streams. It is not just any morning, but *a glorious morning*, and it makes the mountain tops look even better than usual. Alchemy was a combination of magic and science thought to enable the creation of precious gold from ordinary metals, and the excerpt describes the streams as gilded, or covered with gold. The king himself is *kissing with golden face.* The lines are simple, and at the same time, sweet and poetic. The sun is the ruler of all. The writing is fresh and engaging.

Comedic or Tragic Resolution

When an author decides to include a comedic or tragic resolution in a story, the author is using a time-tested literary form that has existed for hundreds, even thousands, of years. The tragedy has a strict format. There is a tragic hero or protagonist who has a fatal flaw and becomes victim to it in the end. The play or story always ends sadly, with the hero in most cases dying or coming to some terrible end. A comedic resolution, on the other hand, always includes a happy ending. There are playful aspects to the plot and the ways in which the characters interact. These literary forms tell the reader what to expect in the story and how to assess the plot. They act as signposts as a reader proceeds through a text.

Understatement or a Sense of Irony

Many authors enjoy using a sense of irony or understatement as they write a story. Both techniques distance the writer from the characters and the events of a story. In either case, the reader must read between the lines to figure out what the author is actually getting at and what his or her point of view actually is. Understatement can be used as a humorous vehicle, allowing the author to comment on what is happening without being deeply emotionally invested in it. Irony allows the author to make a statement about what is really occurring without openly stating it. When reading a text, be sure to look for any underlying meaning that an author might be trying to convey. An initial reading of a text may not be enough to discern its true intended meaning. The way an author talks about what is happening often conveys that author's viewpoint of the events.

Satire vs. Sarcasm

Satire exposes the follies, foibles, and traditions of society, and is often humorous. A satire critiques the pretensions of powerful people in society. While criticism is intended, it is not overt, but rather implied. Mark Twain often employed satire to make a comment about the society in which his characters lived. Sarcasm is a type of humor that is meant to be insulting. Satire may employ the literary technique of irony, which is the tension between what is expected and what actually happens. Sarcasm is a sharp, bitter comment or remark that may or may not utilize understatement. It is an obvious criticism, and does not have the sophistication or creativity of satire, which is usually associated with an entire work. Sarcasm is usually limited to a comment.

Distinguishing Between an Author's Point of View and What They May Say Literarily About a Character or a Situation

An author may use a wide array of literary techniques to discuss a topic, a character, or a situation, which could disguise the author's real feelings regarding what he or she is writing about. For instance, a writer might say that an area received a "little rain," when in fact the land might be flooded with water. Or, an author could describe a dent as "a little scratch" when there is actually an enormous dent. A reader must be able to put a writer's words into perspective to determine what has actually occurred.

The same is true when a writer uses irony to make a comment. Consider the following sentence: "I have little doubt that you will receive the praise that you deserve for your hard work." Taken at face

value, this would be a compliment. However, if the situation is such that the recipient of the comment has made a complete fool of himself, the comment becomes irony, because the opposite of what is being said is true. Here again, the reader has to be careful to examine a situation described by a writer before jumping to conclusions about the author's viewpoint.

WAYS IN WHICH SHAKESPEARE'S *ROMEO AND JULIET* IS A TIMELESS STORY

The story of a young man and woman falling in love and coming to a tragic end has been told over and over, and it represents a universal theme in literature. It was originally told by the Roman writer Ovid in his play *Pyramus and Thisbe*, which is a story of forbidden love. In modern times, a musical with a plot similar to *Romeo and Juliet* is *West Side Story*, which was in fact based on Shakespeare's play. It's important to note, however, that the theme was explored even before Shakespeare wrote his tragedy. Universal themes are found throughout literature. Even the Disney movie *Lady and the Tramp* has elements of the story of ill-fated love that is recounted in *Romeo and Juliet.*

> In what way is *Antigone* by the Greek writer Sophocles related to Henry David Thoreau's essay "Civil Disobedience"? In *Antigone*, the title character defies Creon, the ruler of Thebes, by invoking divine justice and breaking Creon's law to bury her brother. In his essay, Thoreau argues that people have a right and responsibility to rebel against laws that are immoral.

They are related because they share a universal theme of rebelliousness against laws that are unjust. Much of literature contains universal themes that repeat situations and ideals that humans live by. The fact that Antigone went against Creon shows that she had moral courage; the same is true of Thoreau, who argued against laws that were unjust. Even though *Antigone* is a play and was written long ago, it still relates to Thoreau's essay, which was written in the 19th century. Universal themes are timeless and are often repeated, but the context in which they are presented is affected by the times in which they are written.

BOTH HENRY DAVID THOREAU AND NATHANIEL HAWTHORNE WERE AMERICAN WRITERS OF THE 19TH CENTURY. THOREAU'S ESSAYS FOCUSED ON THE QUIET DESPERATION OF MAN. HAWTHORNE'S NOVELS FOCUSED ON CHARACTERS WHO WERE STRUGGLING WITH THE PURITANICAL BACKGROUND OF AMERICA. DISCUSS THE WAYS IN WHICH THEIR VIEWPOINTS WERE DIFFERENT.

Thoreau was part of the Transcendental Movement that was awakening during the 19th century. It held that nature was a vital part of the human experience. Unlike the Puritanical viewpoint that people had little control over their destiny, the Transcendentalists believed that humans could choose their destiny. Thoreau was writing from this viewpoint, while Hawthorne was more concerned with the Puritanical legacy, which allowed little room for change or imagination. His books were a comment on this strict background, while Thoreau's essays were an exploration of a new world. Even though they wrote during the same century, their works represented different understandings of man's position in the universe.

UPTON SINCLAIR'S NOVEL THE JUNGLE IS ABOUT AN IMMIGRANT FAMILY'S EXPERIENCES WORKING IN A FACTORY; JOHN STEINBECK'S NOVEL THE GRAPES OF WRATH IS ABOUT A FAMILY OF MIGRANT WORKERS SUFFERING IN THE DUST BOWL OF MIDDLE AMERICA. THEY WERE BOTH WRITTEN IN THE EARLY 20TH CENTURY. DISCUSS WHY THESE AUTHORS MOST LIKELY DECIDED TO WRITE ABOUT THESE SUBJECTS.

These authors wrote about poor people in difficult situations; they were both concerned about social problems. This is a common theme of early 20th century literature, when the concept of helping the poor worker was just being introduced. One writer spoke of an immigrant family. The other based his novel on a migrant family. They would have had a lot in common, since both families were without roots. This theme is typical of the literature of the early 20th century, when so

many immigrants were pouring into the United States. It was also timely because there were few laws restricting the kind of work that migrants could do

IMPORTANCE OF BEING ABLE TO READ AND COMPREHEND A WIDE VARIETY OF TEXTS BY THE END OF GRADE 11 AND GRADE 12

It is important for an 11th grader to be able to read and comprehend literature—including stories, dramas, and poetry—in order to be well-versed in literature and how it reflects the various periods in which it was written. The student will develop a good background in the cultural aspects of writing, and will know how to respond to cultural references found in texts. The ability to read and comprehend literature will also help the student prepare for his or her future academic and career path.

The reasons why it is important for a student to be able to comprehend a wide variety of texts by the end of the 12th grade are manifold. This background will give the student a great advantage in terms of achieving success in school and the business world. Being widely read ensures greater knowledge of the world, helps a student become well-versed in cultural differences, and also gives the student a chance to develop his or her vocabulary and ability to express her or himself. Ultimately, having read a large number of different literary books will educate the student in many fields, and will help her or him become confident in our ever-complicated world, where communication is vital.

Informational Texts

Inference

An inference is a conclusion you can make based on the evidence in a passage. For instance, if a passage says that there are many people who ride bicycles to work, and that many people prefer riding a bike to driving a car, you might make the conclusion that riding a bike is fun. This is based on the information that you have on hand; it could be wrong, but it is the best guess you can make. Inferences need to have evidence that they are the most likely outcome. In this case, the fact that many people prefer riding a bike to work over driving a car leads the reader to conclude that riding a bike is fun.

Identify the information in the following excerpt that supports the inference that aluminum is a good material for a boat.

> Cement is heavy, and it can support weight. But, it sinks in water. Aluminum is light, and it does not rust easily. It floats easily. Bricks are made up of clay that is fired. They are fire resistant, and they last a long time. But, bricks are heavy.

The information that supports the inference that aluminum is a good material for a boat is that it is light and does not rust easily. Another supporting detail is that it floats easily. This is what the excerpt says. And this is the kind of evidence that is needed to support the inference identified in the question. The other details describe other materials, but they do not give information that suggests these materials would be good for a boat. Inferences are the best conclusions that can be made based on the information at hand.

Determining the Central Ideas of a Passage

Central ideas are what a passage is mainly about. They are why the passage is written. The main idea is often found in a topic sentence or even a concluding sentence, and there are supporting details found in the passage that expand upon the main idea. There can, however, be more than one central idea, and these main ideas can be related and intertwined. For instance, the main or central idea of a passage may be that rainforests are drying out. A related main idea might be that the result of rainforest destruction is a loss of wildlife. These two central ideas are obviously related, and the passage may present both of them by focusing on one in one part of the passage and the other in another part of the passage. Another way they could be related is in a cause and effect relationship, with the loss of rainforests being the reason for losses of wildlife. It is important to always check to see if there is more than one central idea in a passage.

Read the excerpt below. Identify and discuss the main idea.

> Students who have jobs while attending high school tend not to have as much time to complete their homework as other students. They also do not have time for other activities. We should try to persuade our young people to concentrate on doing well in school, not to concentrate on making money. Having a job while you are a student is harmful.

The main idea of the excerpt is actually the last sentence: "Having a job while you are a student is harmful." This is what the excerpt is mostly about. The other sentences contain supporting information: students who have jobs don't have as much time for homework; students with jobs don't have time for as many activities. These are both supporting details that tell more about the main idea. The third sentence deals with a persuasive argument; it is another kind of detail. Only the last sentence tells what the excerpt is mostly about. Main ideas are sometimes found in a topic sentence at the start of a text or in the concluding sentence, which is the case in this excerpt.

Summary of an Informational Text

A summary of an informational text should include the main idea or ideas of the passage and also the pertinent supporting details. A summary should not be a vague statement about what a passage is about, but should include important facts, events, or evidence that make the text a complete work. In order to write an objective summary, you need to think about what the text is saying, and then create a precise outline of the main idea and the important supporting information. Summarizing is not the same as paraphrasing. Paraphrasing involves rewording the main idea and supporting ideas in a fairly detailed way; summarizing does not. Summaries afford the reader the opportunity to quickly review the main points of a passage and the important details.

Analyzing a Text

When you read a text, you need to pay attention. You need to watch for the introduction of ideas. You need to figure out how the ideas that are introduced are developed. When you read a complex text, it may be difficult to follow. Sometimes, it is hard to understand how one idea is linked to another idea. Sometimes, it helps to make an outline of a text. This will help you identify the main ideas. Then, you can figure out which ideas are supporting details. A complex text may also have vocabulary that you cannot understand. If you cannot figure out the meaning of certain words from the context, you can make a list of these words. Then, look them up in a dictionary. This will help you understand the meaning of the text.

Even an informational text tells a story. It introduces information, ideas, individuals, or events, and then provides details about them. A careful reader must learn to figure out the relationships between the details that an author includes and the ideas that the author introduced earlier in the text. Some of the information that is added may be used to supplement the description of an individual, an event, or an idea. Other information may be used to criticize an event, an idea, or an individual. It is up to the reader to have a discerning eye and decide what direction an author is taking by analyzing the author's language and viewpoint, as well as other information.

Meaning of Words and Phrases

The meaning of words and phrases can typically be determined from the context of the sentence in which they appear, as well as the surrounding sentences. It may be necessary to read an entire text to figure out the meaning of a term, particularly a technical or legal term. While words may be used in a literal manner, phrases can be more difficult to figure out since their meaning is often not tied to the exact meaning of the words that comprise them. Phrases are often expressions that need to be interpreted. Expressions are idioms that are usually part of the vernacular of a language. They may require more effort to understand, although the meaning can often still be gleaned from the context.

Discuss the meaning of the phrase "jump ship" in the following sentence.

> The start-up company wasn't working out the way that Hal and his partner hoped, and they thought it was time to jump ship and get into another business.

To figure out the meaning of the phrase "jump ship," the reader needs to look for context clues in the same way he or she would to figure out the meaning of a single word. The sentence says that the start-up company wasn't working out. It says that Hal and his partner thought it was time to get into another business. You can tell from the context of the sentence that the expression "jump ship" means to get out of something or to quit something. It has nautical overtones, and it comes from a nautical saying, but the context of the sentence makes it clear what the expression, or idiom, means. Although it might seem to have negative connotations, it does not necessarily have to be negative. It is a kind of final act, which could be construed as negative. However, the context of the sentence suggests that "jumping ship" in this instance might result in something positive occurring.

READ THE EXCERPT BELOW. USE THE CONTEXT CLUES TO DECIDE WHAT THE WORD "WATERLOO" MEANS IN THIS INSTANCE.

> Connie was worried that the competition was her Waterloo. She realized she wasn't Napoleon and she wasn't losing her entire kingdom because she lost a battle, but that's how it felt to her.

Using context clues is a good way to figure out the meanings of words and expressions without having to look them up in a dictionary. The way to discover context clues is to study the text. The excerpt says that Connie was worried that the competition was her Waterloo. This is obviously a reference to something, but it takes further analysis to figure out what it means. The next sentence talks about Napoleon and how he lost a kingdom because of a battle. One can draw the conclusion that "Waterloo" was probably the battle, and that someone's Waterloo is something that a person loses or does badly in. This helps the reader figure out the meaning of the word.

FIGURATIVE LANGUAGE

Figurative language is language that is used in a non-literal way. It allows the writer to expand the ways in which he or she uses language, making it more colorful and fresh. Figurative language takes a word or an expression that has a literal meaning and gives it a new one. For instance, an author might say that Lilli is like a graceful swan. While everyone knows that Lilli is a person, the image of Lilli as a graceful swan casts a new descriptive meaning. Figurative language takes many forms; it can be in the form of a simile, a metaphor, personification, or hyperbole. Similes compare things using the comparing words "*like*" or "*as.*" An example is, "Lilli is like a graceful swan." Metaphors compare things without using comparing words. An example is, "Lilli is a swan when she moves." Personification attributes human traits to an animal or an inanimate object. An example is, "The swan spoke to Lilli."

READ THE EXCERPT FROM FORMER PRESIDENT GEORGE W. BUSH'S SECOND INAUGURAL ADDRESS.

> "...By our efforts, we have lit a fire as well - a fire in the minds of men. It warms those who feel its power, it burns those who fight its progress, and one day this untamed fire of freedom will reach the darkest corners of our world."

DISCUSS THE METAPHOR THAT FORMER PRESIDENT BUSH USES IN THIS EXCERPT.

The metaphor that President Bush uses is that of a fire of freedom that will grow in the minds of men and will warm those who feel its power. This fire is powerful, according to the metaphor, since it would burn those who fight against freedom. It is also powerful because it will reach all over the world. Bush uses the metaphor of a fire since it suggests light, and democracy is a kind of light that allows people to see the truth. That is why the metaphor is a powerful one. This is an example of how strong a metaphor can be in terms of getting a person's viewpoint and thoughts across to the public.

AGGRESSIVE VS. ASSERTIVE CONNOTATIONS

The words "aggressive" and "assertive" both describe someone with a strong nature. However, the word "aggressive" suggests someone who may be hostile or belligerent, while the term "assertive" could be interpreted to mean self-confident or self-assured. "Aggressive" has negative connotations when used to describe someone's nature, while the word "assertive" has more positive connotations. These words are examples of differences in connotations, since they both have meanings that go beyond what appears in the dictionary. Words like these should be chosen carefully, since they can convey a message about someone that may or may not be intended. When choosing words, a writer needs to look for the most accurate word to describe a person or a thing.

Author's Point of View

When an author writes a text, he or she must choose the structure that will work best for the text. For informational passages, there are several different structures an author can use. These include question and answer order, chronological or sequential order, problem and solution order, cause and effect order, and spatial order. Some texts use a combination of two or more of these structures depending on the breakdown of the topic. For persuasive documents, a question and answer order is often a good choice because it allows for a dramatic presentation of materials. This structure allows the author to highlight arguments for or against a position. A cause and effect order structure might also be a good choice for a persuasive text, and would also allow for the highlighting of arguments, as would a problem and solution order. Compare and contrast and order of importance are reasonable choices for informational pieces, and possibly for persuasive texts as well. Chronological ordering would be more suitable for an informational piece on a person or an event, where the points that are being made are not meant to convince the reader of something. The author should choose the structure that will best meet his or her writing goals.

Veronica is doing a report on why people should stop the killing of whales. She is trying to figure out which text structure would best help her meet her goal to outline the reasons why this harvesting will result in the loss of species that are important to the environment. Describe which type of order would probably work best for this report, and explain why.

The best possible choices for the report would probably be either a problem and solution or a cause and effect organization, since they would allow the author to lay out the problem and the consequences of the killing of whales. A cause and effect order would show the immediate relationship between the killing of whales and its consequence; a problem and solution order would probably be best if the author wants to concentrate on the ways in which this practice is causing society problems and how the practice could be resolved. A compare and contrast structure would probably not work in this type of report. Finally, a chronological structure, which might be useful in part of the report to outline the past history of the practice, would probably not be a suitable structure for the entire report.

An author's point of view may be clear, or it may be hidden. It is important to read a text closely to find out exactly what the author thinks about the event, person, topic, or issue he or she is writing about. When reading, look for clues to the author's viewpoint in the form of emotional statements or critiques of others discussing the topic. Some authors make their viewpoints known only through rhetorical statements. These need to be analyzed closely to see if they should be taken at face value or if the author is somehow using rhetoric to exaggerate a point or to try to persuade the reader of something. Rhetoric can be a very effective vehicle that can draw a reader in through the use of elegant language. This is precisely why it is important to analyze an author's rhetoric to determine why he or she is employing it and what his or her goal might be. It is also vital to read the entire text before making any assumptions about an author's viewpoint.

The purpose of the rhetoric in the following excerpt from a speech by former President George W. Bush.

> "Our opportunities are too great, our lives too short, to waste this moment. So tonight we vow to our nation. We will seize this moment of American promise. We will use these good times for great goals."

The President's purpose is clear; he wants to set an important goal for the public. In doing so, he is attempting to paint a picture of the importance of what he is saying. Phrases such as "Our opportunities are too great," "We will seize the moment," and "good times for great goals" set the stage for putting forth the President's agenda, which he hopes to present in the best possible light. Words have the capacity to transfix listeners with their elegance, a fact clearly illustrated by this excerpt. That is why speeches are so important to the political arena, and it is why excellent speech writers are extremely important to political candidates.

Using Information Technology Skills Wisely

Good information technology skills are necessary in order to sift through the enormous amount of information available on just about any topic. Before beginning any research, ask yourself how much information you think you are going to need; think about your target audience and their needs. Utilize search engines to make the task go faster. When evaluating multiple sources of information, do not rely solely on how recent they are. Consider the validity of sources as well. Do not rely on just one source. Using digital media is important because it allows you to broaden your scope beyond just words to include graphics and charts. Take the time to understand what online sources of information are available, which ones are most appropriate, and how they support one another.

Using the reasoning that the Founding Fathers believed that African Americans could not be viewed as citizens as defined in the US Constitution, and therefore had no rights before the Court, Chief Justice Taney's majority opinion ignited a firestorm of controversy in the already heated debate between pro- and anti-slavery advocates in the United States during the mid-19th century. Many opponents decried the Chief Justice's ruling as one that was motivated by politics. One result was that the US Congress could no longer regulate slavery anywhere. The Dred Scott Decision is viewed as one of a series of events that eventually pushed the country into the Civil War.

Analyze the following excerpt from Lincoln's Second Inaugural Address in 1865.

> "It may seem strange that any men should dare to ask a just God's assistance in wringing their bread from the sweat of other men's faces, but let us judge not, that we be not judged. The prayers of both could not be answered. That of neither has been answered fully..."

In this excerpt and in the address, Lincoln is talking about slavery. Like the majority of people of his time, Lincoln learned to read by studying the Bible. He makes frequent references to the Bible, and he often uses the rhetoric of the Bible to drive his point home. This is common in 19th century literary documents. When he says, "Wringing their bread from the sweat of other men's faces," he is paraphrasing from the Book of Genesis, which refers to physical work. Here, the word *bread* is used to refer to the wealth of the slave owners. Lincoln finds it strange that these slave owners should pray to the same God as those who do not own slaves for assistance in making money. He encourages his audience not to be hypocritical when he says, "let us judge not." This is a reference to the Book of Matthew of the Bible.

Importance of Being a Proficient Reader of Literary Nonfiction Texts by Grade 11 and Grade 12

It is extremely important for a student to be proficient in reading literary nonfiction texts by the end of grade 11. These types of texts will play a key role in the student's future life (and success). In other words, the ability to comprehend language and vocabulary will help the student attain the academic level he or she hopes to or the type of employment desired. In all walks of life, people need to be able to read and comprehend a variety of materials. This is why the ability to understand literary nonfiction texts is a valuable tool. It is especially important for those who hope to do well on college entrance examinations as well as other kinds of job examinations.

It is of the utmost importance for a 12th-grade student to be able to read literary nonfiction proficiently. Not only is it important for future academic endeavors (e.g., college and graduate school), but it is also vital to future career success. Whether it is reading a newspaper, an employee manual, or a science text, it is crucial that a person be comfortable when reading and be able to comprehend the material without extreme effort. Without this ability, a person will face limitations in his or her academia and business life. Communication is extremely important in today's workplace, and the foundation of this skill is being able to comprehend reading materials.

UNIVERSAL THEMES FOUND IN LITERATURE ARE AFFECTED BY THE TIME IN WHICH THE LITERATURE WAS WRITTEN

While universal themes are the same in terms of their meaning and what they depict or teach, the ways in which they are presented are affected by the time in which a literary piece was written. The characters and situations that are portrayed will mirror the environment in which the writer lived. Ancient literature depicts a time when myth was very much alive, and when the concept of personal freedom was still evolving and not taken for granted.

EVALUATE THE PURPOSE OF THE FOLLOWING EXCERPT FROM GEORGE WASHINGTON'S FAREWELL ADDRESS, WHICH WAS GIVEN ON SEPTEMBER 19, 1796.

> "The unity of government which constitutes you one people is also now dear to you. It is justly so, for it is a main pillar in the edifice of your real independence, the support of your tranquility at home, your peace abroad; of your safety; of your prosperity; of that very liberty which you so highly prize..."

This address given by the first president of the US when he announced that he did not want to run for re-election went over the groundwork that had established the new country. The passage stresses *the unity of government which constitutes you one people.* Washington truly believed that the US would be able to survive any attack, from without as well as from within, if it stayed with this principle. There is a hint that Washington foresaw the difficulties of holding together *the main pillar* (the different states) that were to come. His farewell address would go on to influence politicians and leaders for many years to come.

Writing

Clear and Coherent Writing

Clear and coherent writing requires good initial planning. You need to determine what you are going to say, who you are saying it to, and how you want to say it, as well as the kind of tone you want to project. In the process of writing, organize your arguments and use a logical order to develop them. Use paragraph breaks to help organize your thoughts. Your sentences should be precise and to the point. Make sure your punctuation is correct. Your ideas should be supported by evidence, and opposing ideas should be mentioned as well. When you get to your conclusion, avoid being repetitious; concentrate on summarizing. Proofread what you have written to check for any errors; reading the text aloud is often helpful.

Importance of Planning, Revising, Editing, and Reviewing a Text

Draw up a brief plan before you start to write so that you know what points you are going to cover. Once you have finished the writing, it is a good idea to set it aside for a time. That way, when you look at it again to see if revisions are needed, you will be approaching it with a fresh mind. During the process of editing, make sure you check for any grammatical, spelling, punctuation, or usage errors. Are your supporting details clear and presented in a logical order? Will your audience respond to your text? During your review process, you may feel that some sections need to be rewritten. Think about whatever criticism your peers or adults may have had about previous work as you review your writing.

Read the following passage, explain why it needs to be revised, and discuss how best to revise it.

> Raising a puppy is more difficult. We all know how cute they are. Like kittens, they need a lot of care. So, don't be shocked that I tell you kittens are more cute.

The writer of these sentences has not made it clear what he or she is really trying to say. There is no organization, and there are grammatical and usage errors. A good revision would look like this:

> We all know how cute puppies and kittens are. They both require a lot of care, but I think puppies are more difficult to raise than kittens. I also think that kittens are cuter than puppies.

Here the thoughts are put down in a logical order. The writer makes a statement of fact (*puppies and kittens are cute*), and one of opinion (*I think...*), so it is clear what her preferences are. The passage now makes sense, and the writing is free from errors.

Conducting a Research Project

When conducting a short or a sustained research project to answer a question or solve a problem, it is a good idea to draw up a plan first. Then, make a list of keywords related to the question or problem. You can utilize these words either in a search engine or an online or print encyclopedia. Back issues of magazines, journals, and newspapers can also be used as source material. If you are synthesizing multiple sources, combine the similarities or the differences you have come up with. It is important that none of the information you gather be dated or untimely. All sources have to be cited following Modern Language Association (MLA) guidelines. Questions raised by your research should be explicit.

USING THE INTERNET

Online sources that allow writers to get works published at little to no cost either as an e-book or a printed book are now widely available. There are editing as well as marketing services offered on many Internet sites. Writing tools offer help with everything from style to grammar. Sites for research are reliable, and offer accurate and objective information. Make sure you cite Internet sources using an accepted format such as that from the MLA (Modern Language Association). There are free online tools that can be accessed to allow people to work together on projects no matter how far apart they are geographically. Chat rooms and topic websites allow for an unprecedented exchange of information. Shared writing projects let you get adult input or brainstorm with your peers.

GATHERING RELEVANT INFORMATION FROM MULTIPLE PRINT AND DIGITAL SOURCES

Before compiling information from multiple print and digital sources, you must first decide how much information you need based on the scope of the project, and you must determine how knowledgeable your audience is. Make an outline of the similarities as well as the differences you encounter in various sources. Journals, text books, magazines, newspapers, and even texts written by other students: the number of sources you can uncover is limited only by your imagination. Strike a balance between being too detailed and bogged down, and too general and oversimplified. Whatever the source, verify how timely, accurate, and credible it is. You can avoid plagiarism, or using another person's words without acknowledgement, by following MLA (Modern Language Association) guidelines when you cite their works.

F. *Scott Fitzgerald's novel The Great Gatsby takes place on Long Island (near New York City) in the 1920s, during an era known as the Jazz Age. Discuss what the author's subject reveals about American society at that time.*

Fitzgerald was writing about a time when there was a period of great wealth in the country, as well as great excess and abandon, after the end of World War I. He portrays society's fascination with the ideals of wealth and happiness, the so-called "American Dream." The two main characters, Nick and Gatsby, both of whom served their country during the war, are cynical and disillusioned. Gatsby throws lavish parties at his estate every weekend with liquor (outlawed by the Eighteenth Amendment) flowing freely. Fitzgerald captures the mood with striking clarity, portraying the moral emptiness of the time and the growing distrust of the wealthy as the decade careened towards its close with the Great Depression of 1929.

EVALUATE THE PURPOSE OF THE FOLLOWING EXCERPT FROM FRANKLIN D. ROOSEVELT'S SPEECH OF JULY 2, 1932.

> "I pledge you, I pledge myself, to a new deal for the American people. Let us all here assembled constitute ourselves prophets of a new order of competence and of courage. This is more than a political campaign; it is a call to arms..."

In this speech given by Franklin D. Roosevelt when he accepted the Democratic nomination for President, he proposed launching a new effort to turn back the tide of Depression that had gripped the country for several years. In using the phrase "a call to arms," he addressed the audience in a manner similar to how a commander would address his soldiers. His purpose was to contrast himself and the Democratic Party with the Republican view of government, which favored big businesses and a continuation of the policies of Herbert Hoover. He subsequently went on to win in a landslide victory in November, and his policies, of course, went on to be labeled by history as The New Deal.

MAKE WRITING A HABIT

In today's information driven society, writing is a skill that is of utmost importance in adult life. Writing, whether it is a short paragraph or two or an extended thesis, should come easily and smoothly (and should even be second nature) for those who wish to be successful. As such, writing should become a habit. An adult who follows the old adage "the more you write, the better you write" is sure to achieve recognition in any field of endeavor. It is important to study the writing process—the conscious effort of note taking, writing drafts, editing, and revising—so that you will grasp the concept of fine tuning your writing to different audiences, and will feel equally at ease writing a short note or a thoroughly researched treatise.

Persuasive text

Introducing an Argument in a Persuasive Passage

The best way to introduce an argument in a persuasive passage and to structure it is to begin by organizing your thoughts and researching the evidence carefully. You should write everything down in outline format to start. Make sure you put the claim at the beginning of the passage. Then, list the reasons and the evidence that you have to support the claim. It is important that you provide enough evidence. Reasons and evidence should follow each other in a logical order. Write the passage so that you hold the reader's attention; use a strong tone and choose words carefully for maximum effect. If you can get the reader to understand your claim, he or she will be more likely to agree with your argument. Restate your claim in the concluding paragraph to maximize the impact on the reader.

Making a Claim

When making a claim, it is important to first think about the arguments that support that claim. While researching, try to anticipate what readers might say; this will help you thoroughly develop your claim. It is not enough to research a claim on the Internet, because many sources are dubious at best. Look for sites that are objective. Find authorities that you can quote, and use statistics. Present counterclaims using ample evidence. Mention both the strengths and weaknesses without any prejudice. Divide each counterclaim into a separate paragraph with supporting evidence. Make sure to present everything in a logical manner so that the information will be easily understood by the reader. Most importantly, one needs to separate opinions from facts.

Creating Cohesion

The best way to create cohesion between claims and evidence is to organize your ideas, and then write sentences explaining your reasons and evidence that logically follow your main ideas. Careful research will result in your argument being cohesive and easy to understand. Your claim and evidence must be clearly related to each other. Sometimes, it is useful to include metaphors, similes, or analogies to make your point clearer. Words and phrases that will indicate to the reader that the claim and evidence are related include "since," "because," "as a consequence," and "as a result." You can also utilize clauses to demonstrate a relationship between the reason and the effect. This approach is illustrated in the following sentence: "Since the sun now rose earlier in the morning, the birds awakened earlier and began their song." The first clause sets the tone, and it establishes causality between the reason and the effect. After writing, reread your text to verify that the relationships between cause and effect are logical.

Formal Style

A formal style is important when you want your writing to be objective and precise. A few requirements must be met to achieve this. It is important not to use fragments; write in complete sentences. Avoid contractions, and do not change tenses between sentences or paragraphs. Do not use the words "I" or "you"; this will add a more serious tone to your writing. Whenever possible, avoid using the passive tense. Using the active voice will make your writing more focused and interesting. Ensure your spelling is correct and that you follow all punctuation rules. Finally, make sure your ideas are presented in a logical order.

READ THE FOLLOWING PASSAGE AND SUGGEST SOME WAYS TO MAKE IT MORE FORMAL.

> When I was a kid growing up, I remember I had a lot of hard times. As a teenager, other kids used to make fun of me and call me names. It was really depressing. I couldn't find anyone to take to the prom. Sometimes, it was hard to keep up with all my homework.

HERE IS ONE WAY TO REWRITE IT:

> Becoming a teenager can be a stressful time. Adolescence involves both physical and emotional changes. Peer pressure and pressure at school cause many teenagers to have anxiety disorders; some even suffer from mild to severe depression. Boys and girls both worry about their physical appearance and about being popular.

The account is presented in the third person to make the passage more authoritative and formal. Complex sentences are utilized to keep the writing varied and interesting. Personal emotions are expressed in a more objective manner. A higher level of vocabulary results in a more precise, informed, and impressive finished text.

CONCLUDING STATEMENT

A concluding statement is an important part of a persuasive passage because it sets the tone for the reader and adds a sense of completion. A concluding sentence should not just repeat what was already said; the concluding statement should tie everything together. The concluding sentence should basically restate the importance of the argument. By doing this in the concluding paragraph, the impact on the reader will be maximized, and you will be more likely to bring the reader over to your side of an argument. The conclusion should logically fit into the flow of your passage. A good concluding statement serves to cement the bonds you have developed with the reader, and provides one more opportunity to get the reader on your side.

WHAT KIND OF ARGUMENT WOULD THE FOLLOWING CONCLUDING SENTENCE BE BEST SUITED FOR?

> As a result, soccer is the most popular sport in the world.

The sentence makes a good concluding sentence for a passage about the reasons why soccer (called football outside of the US) is the most popular sport in the world. Arguments can include the fact that players do not need any special equipment, while players of a similar sport—American football—need equipment such as helmets and protective padding. Another good angle is the fact that players don't have to be a certain size to play soccer, whereas the sport of American football places a premium on very large players, especially when filling defensive positions. Basketball, another sport that is also popular, requires a wooden court and two metal baskets with nets installed at a certain height. The concluding sentence provided would tie all the elements of the argument together.

Informational or Explanatory Text

Introducing a Topic

An informational or explanatory text should have an introduction to the topic that the text will cover. One way you can accomplish this is by using a topic sentence, with details that support your thesis included afterwards. Another tactic is to use a reference to something going on in the modern world, even if your topic relates to something in the past. This makes your topic immediately more relevant. Some writers like to preview the ideas and concepts they are going to discuss by showing their relevance to a main topic. You could also preview concepts by demonstrating how they relate to everyday life.

Developing a Topic

It is important to develop the topic of an informational or explanatory text by utilizing relevant facts that clearly support the main topic. Include a topic sentence followed by any supporting details. These details should preferably be concrete facts that you have carefully researched, and which you are certain are accurate. You can also provide quotes taken from known experts in a field that is relevant to your topic. Quotes not only lend credibility to your thesis, but can also make your writing more varied and interesting. Diverse multimedia techniques, charts, and examples will also enhance your presentation. However, you should make sure these techniques play a supportive role, and are not presented solely to make your text look flashy.

Creating Cohesion

Experienced writers know how to use appropriate transitions to create cohesion in a text. They serve to clarify the relationships between ideas and concepts. Transition words or phrases such as "consequently," "therefore," and "as a result of" indicate causality between ideas. "However," "on the other hand," "in contrast," "but," and "similarly" indicate a compare and contrast relationship. You can also draw attention to examples by using words and phrases like "namely," "for example," "for instance," and "that is." When you need to show the order of importance of ideas or concepts, use transitions such as "at first," "primarily," "secondly," "former," or "latter."

Using Precise Language and Domain-Specific Vocabulary

Writers of informational or explanatory texts must use precise language and domain specific vocabulary in order to accurately get their ideas across. General vocabulary words will not bring home the points you are trying to make. Your audience will not follow your thesis closely if the text lacks the details that are supplied by carefully chosen, precise, and domain specific language. Using the word "isobar" in a text about meteorology, for instance, would be more effective than using the word "pressure." During the research stage, make sure you closely study the vocabulary used. Use a dictionary to clarify the meanings of words and terms you do not understand.

Establishing and Maintaining a Formal Style

Experienced writers use a formal style when they are writing explanatory or informational texts to lend greater credence to their material. They do not use an informal or colloquial tone, and they utilize the third person for objectivity. They use complex sentences, which are longer and add a further tone of formality and depth to the subject. By using a formal style, they show that they are serious about their subject. They are striving to make supporting details clear and to the point, but they are also presenting them in as much complexity as the intended audience can absorb. There is no introduction of personal opinion, unless that opinion can be carefully justified.

Importance of a Good Concluding Statement

A good concluding statement should sum up the overall intention of the text, and serves to "wrap up" the passage so that the reader is aware that you arrived at the logical ending of your argument. The conclusion should review the most salient points that you made, the reasoning you employed, and the supporting arguments for your reasoning. It serves to reinforce in the reader's mind that you did not leave anything out. The reader should not feel that there is more pertinent information that may follow. A good conclusion allows the reader to sit back and weigh the overall impact of your thesis, and it greatly increases the effectiveness of a text.

Narratives

SETTING THE STAGE

To set the stage for a narrative, you need to introduce the reader to the setting and the characters. Next, you should introduce a plot line. This should consist of various events that lead to a problem, a climax, and a resolution. This gives a narrative structure. The way in which the author introduces these elements has an influence on the overall effectiveness of the narrative. Make sure to use language to describe the setting and the characters that will grab the reader's attention. Make the details specific. The conclusion or resolution will allow you to tie up the details of the story.

INTRODUCING A NARRATOR

The narrator in a story is the person doing the "speaking," or the one who is telling the story. A narrator can speak in the first or third person. The narrator can shift from one person to another during the course of the story. It is even possible for the narrator to be non-human. The introduction of your narrator can be quick, subtle, dramatic, or humorous; it is up to you. Many times, an event or a circumstance opens the story. Make sure any details about time, place, and circumstance are developed logically and naturally, and that the reader will understand who (or what) the narrator is and where the narrator fits into the story.

USING TECHNIQUES

Writers employ numerous techniques to bring a narrative to life. Dialogue is one tool; it gives the reader a sense of what is happening, and also adds color and nuance to characters or the narrator. What a character says and how he says it portrays how that character feels. Pacing is also used in a narrative. The rhythms of the sentences, whether they are short or long, allow a writer to use time to the best effect, and to add color and depth to the events in the narrative. The plot line or sequence of events in the narrative is the actual structure of the story, and is developed from the opening of the story through one or more actions. These actions eventually lead to a climax, and then a resolution. The use of descriptions lets the reader visualize what is happening.

INTERJECTING SEQUENCE

Sequence should come in an order that can be easily grasped by the reader. It is a function of a natural flow of events, dialogue, and plot. Sequence should enhance what is happening in the story, and it should never seem forced or unnatural. A pattern should emerge, and it must make sense to the reader. Often times, a writer will make use of a flashback, a literary device where the writer goes back in time, and where events do not follow in sequence. When crafted properly, the flashback will make sense in the context of the story. Flashbacks can often add a sense of mystery or suspense to a narrative. Chronological narration, which puts events in the order in which they happened, is another literary device, and is used more frequently than flashbacks.

USING PRECISE LANGUAGE

Precise language is important in a narrative. It helps ensure that the concepts you are trying to communicate are readily understood by the audience. Precise language will be livelier, and will provoke more thought on the part of the reader. It includes the proper use of dialogue and imagery to get the point of the story across as succinctly as possible, so that there is nothing vague in the narrative. Your use of language should show an articulate grasp and control of the plot, and the whole text should be cohesive. Sensory language (which brings up images of the senses) can add extra detail and feeling, and can be very persuasive. Understanding the full range of language will result in a better narrative.

Importance of the Conclusion

The conclusion to a narrative is extremely important. An inadequate or poorly thought out conclusion can leave the reader confused and unable to tie everything together, or "wrap things up." There must be some type of resolution to whatever was described in the opening and the events that followed. A conclusion is not repetition; it is resolution. The resolution can be a summary. It could be a quotation. The resolution does not have to be clear cut. In fact, it may leave a lot unanswered. It could end with a rhetorical question or questions. Indeed, unlike traditional writing, conclusions in modern literature often present more questions than answers. In every case, however, the conclusion will leave the reader with no doubt that the narrative is over.

Doreen is writing a short story about training her dog Lola to compete in an agility competition. She has written about all that she has done to train her dog over the past three months. She is preparing to write a conclusion to her story. Describe what Doreen should try to accomplish with her conclusion.

Doreen should write a conclusion to tie everything together. Since she was training her dog Lola to compete, the end of the story should tell whether Lola won the competition. Doreen should describe the day of the competition and the result. This is the most obvious conclusion for her story. Doreen should bring her story to a close with a fitting and appropriate ending so that the reader will know exactly what the outcome was, and will not be left hanging in the end. The opening and all the events that happened lead up to this, and there is a form to her story.

Speaking and Listening

Discussions

Preparing for a Discussion on a Particular Topic

It is exceedingly important to prepare for class discussions. These discussions are important because they help prepare students for future discussions, and also allow them to practice effective techniques and learn communication skills. The exchanging of ideas is a skill that will remain with a student throughout his or her lifetime. When preparing for such a discussion, a student should research the subject at hand using the Internet and other sources. They should make sure they have read all essential applicable information. It is also important to have the resources (quotes, statistics, and audio visual material) you will need during the discussion on hand. A useful technique is to rehearse your role; practice the day before with a family member or a friend. Determine what you are going to focus on. If you are leading the discussion, think ahead about how you are going to guide the discussion to a conclusion, and how much time will be needed.

Rules for Collegial Discussions

Properly organized collegial discussions can be very productive, and can result in many new and interesting ideas being formulated and brought out in the classroom. It is important that rules be set up to promote civil, democratic discussions. Guidelines for the discussion should be established, which should include how much time each participant will be allowed to talk and then respond. There should be clear roles. Specific goals need to be established, and the progress towards reaching those goals should be tracked, with a deadline for completion kept in mind. Participants should learn how to use questions to add detail and depth to the discussion, and how to build on and further ideas that are put forth by others. It is important to try to understand and communicate with individuals who have a different perspective, especially from a cultural point of view. Everyone should be able to make use of evidence, and should be able to express themselves clearly within the structured framework.

Ways to Pose Questions That Elicit Elaboration

Asking questions that will encourage a response from others and propel a conversation entails asking specific, not general, questions, since they force the listener to think. Ideally, questions should be open-ended (i.e. they can't be answered with a simple "yes" or "no"). It is important to be proficient at asking questions, and at learning the art of asking the right question. Being a good listener is key to asking good questions. You should build on the ideas expressed by others in the classroom. One technique is asking a question at the end of what you have to say. You could ask something like, "Does that answer your question?" This helps personalize questions. Another overlooked technique is to take notes. It is also important to prevent people from straying from the subject by taking control of the situation and diplomatically steering the conversation back to the subject at hand.

Ensuring That a Full Range of Positions Are Equally Covered

Guidelines for the discussion should stress allowing each member of the team to express his or her viewpoint without prejudice. Each member should receive the same amount of time to put forth a theory or thesis, or to address a subject through an analytical probe without interruption. On the other hand, every team member should also be granted time to respond to individual presentations. Emotional outbursts do not have a place in this kind of discussion, nor do personal comments that pull away from an objective and intelligent discussion. When there is a divergence of opinion, the greatest of respect should be given to the opposing viewpoints.

Respond to Diverse Perspectives

Key to responding to diverse perspectives is listening and keeping an open mind. Divergent ideas could be compiled by the entire discussion group in a list. Then, the link between the ideas could be identified, and it might be determined through consensus which opinions require more scrutiny or research. A goal should be set for the investigation or task, and assignments made so that any further research that is needed is done. The conversation can then resume with this new additional information kept in mind. This process is an orderly means of reaching a deeper understanding of a topic that not everyone may agree with or about.

Integrating Various Sources of Information That Are Presented in Diverse Formats and Media

There are many different sources of information. On the Internet, there are multiple sites (some more reliable than others) where print information as well as charts and other graphic organizers are available to all. In addition, there are hard copy and online journals, textbooks, magazines, and newspapers; researchers are often overwhelmed with information. It is best to choose only the sources that can be verified or are from a credible author or organization. This information must then be analyzed to see how consistent it is and whether valid discrepancies exist, and why. After, it can be used in a presentation or a discussion.

Analyzing a Speaker's Point of View

The point of view of a speaker needs to be determined to evaluate whether there is a clear delineation between evidence and the speaker's theory. If a speaker's viewpoint is prejudiced or based on emotion, this needs to be identified by evaluating the evidence. It is important to evaluate a speaker's choice of words and tone to determine whether the speech is tinged with feeling or objective. The evidence that a speaker uses to back up claims must also be closely evaluated to determine its source and validity. Many speakers are able to influence an audience through their strength of delivery, but if studied, there may be holes in logic or faults in the evidence that is used to prove a point.

Presenting Claims, Findings, and Supporting Evidence

When in a focused discussion, be prepared to present your claims, findings, and supporting evidence in a clear and distinct manner. This means being prepared. When compiling your data, make sure to create an outline that has the main ideas and then the supporting evidence, including graphics that you want to present. Attention to details will result in a successful presentation, one in which the diverse individuals in the group will come away with a feeling of having been part of something meaningful. Facts and examples should be stressed. Repetition creates retention. It is important for the speaker to choose the right words, and to build momentum by gradually building up to the strongest argument(s). Graphics are important, because participants will be more convinced if they can see evidence as well as hear it. By breaking up the flow of the discussion and introducing pauses before and after pertinent arguments, the speaker will make the presentation of facts more interesting.

Presentations

One way to bring a presentation to life is to use digital media, including graphics, audio, visual, and interactive elements. Such tools will not only make a presentation more interesting and memorable, but will also keep those listening from distancing themselves from the presentation. It is easy for audience members to become bored during a presentation if they don't feel included. Digital media can effectively hold their interest. Graphics, diagrams, charts, and maps all serve to reinforce the point you are trying to make. The simpler these forms of media are, the more effective they will be. They serve to help the audience understand your argument; a video or audio can enhance the claims and findings of a presentation. Both visuals and multimedia components should be considered aids; they are not going to do the work for you. It is useful to rehearse the presentation until it flows smoothly.

When giving a speech, you need to make sure you feel confident in front of your audience. Exchange nerves for a funny story to open; have a variety of multimedia graphics that will pull your audience in. Perhaps most important, use the English language correctly when you speak. This is a situation where using correct grammar is essential. Before you speak, write your speech out and make sure that it demonstrates a command of correct conventions. In addition, be sure to speak clearly and slowly, and to enunciate words. Make sure the words that you choose have the correct literal meaning and the intended connotations. Try to avoid hesitations that end with "uh" or "er," which only distract from what you are saying. Look at one person in the audience and talk to her or him. Maintaining a smile will help create an atmosphere of informality. Extra effort needs to be made to avoid being wordy. Redundancy is sure to make audience attention wander.

Eye contact is one of the most important tactics for an effective presentation. When you maintain eye contact with audience members, you can be assured that your listeners will find your presentation believable. They will also be more likely to remember what you said. Reading a speech instead of giving one will have little impact on your audience. Make sure to look people in the eyes and smile. Use a voice that can be easily heard, and enunciate words so people will not be left wondering what was said. Remember to adapt your voice to the task at hand. Are you trying to persuade, look for sympathy, or tell an amazing story? All of these scenarios should yield a different voice and way of presenting the material. Most important of all, relax!

Language

Usage is a Matter of Convention

Latin is an ancient language. It does not change. But English, like any modern language, may change over time. New words are always being introduced into the English language. Words are adapted from other languages. Examples of adapted words are taco, pizza, and karaoke. Usage, which is a matter of convention, can also change and evolve over time. It is not always clear what the correct form is, since there are sometimes two possibilities. For instance, the use of the subjunctive is much less prevalent today than it was in the past. The answer to the question of whether it is acceptable to begin a question with the word "and" or "but" has also changed. Years ago, this was strictly against usage rules, but it is now common practice in less formal texts.

Use of the Serial Comma

The rules regarding use of the serial comma differ depending on whether a text is academic or more informal. Traditionally, and in academia, a comma is always used before the "and" in a list of items. This is not the case in more casual texts, such as newspapers, where the convention is not to use a comma before the word "and" in a list of items. This is just one example of how usage conventions are not always rigid, and can change according to the usage of the moment. A general rule of thumb is that a comma should be used in front of the "and" in a list of items if the text is for a school-related or academic use, but should not be used if the text is intended for everyday use.

Marina and Keegan are writing a report together. They are having a disagreement about whether a split infinitive Marina used in one sentence is grammatically correct. Marina thinks the split infinitive is fine in this instance, but Keegan does not agree. How can they come to a resolution about this issue?

There are many grey areas related to English usage, and split infinitives is one of them. The strict notion that they should never be used is less in vogue today than it was a few years ago, and they may now even be found in formal writing. However, if the text that is being prepared is academic, it is probably best to avoid using them. In English, it is always possible to word things differently to avoid awkward usage, and this is also true for split infinitives. Marina and Keegan could consult *Merriam-Webster's Dictionary of English Usage* or *Garner's Modern American Usage* to figure out what they should do. Typically, however, the more academic the paper, the more formal the usage should be.

Rules of Hyphenation

Hyphens are used in many instances. They are used to join compound words, whether nouns or verbs. The best way to determine if a word needs a hyphen is to check it in the dictionary. They are used to separate two or more adjectives when they come before a noun. They are used to hyphenate all compound numbers from *twenty-one* through *ninety-nine*. They are used to hyphenate all spelled-out fractions. They are used to hyphenate prefixes when they come before proper nouns. They are used to hyphenate all words beginning with *self* except *selfish* and *selfless*. They are used in some titles, such as vice-president. It is important not to confuse a hyphen with a dash.

Correct the punctuation in the following sentence.

> The forty year old man jumped over the bramble covered fence rail, where he came upon a too good to be true treasure chest filled with gold pieces that were really chocolate candies.

THE CORRECT WAY TO WRITE THIS SENTENCE IS: THE FORTY-YEAR-OLD MAN JUMPED OVER THE BRAMBLE-COVERED FENCE RAIL, WHERE HE CAME UPON A TOO-GOOD-TO-BE-TRUE TREASURE CHEST FILLED WITH GOLD PIECES THAT WERE REALLY CHOCOLATE CANDIES.

Hyphens are used to join several adjectives modifying a noun when they cannot be joined by the word "and." "Forty," "year," and "old" all modify man and are hyphenated; these modifiers cannot be joined by "and." The same is true of "bramble covered." It would be awkward to say bramble and covered. The two words work together to create a description, so they are hyphenated. The last group of adjectives is "too," "good," and "to be true," which is really an expression that needs to be hyphenated. It is important not to confuse a hyphen with a dash; a dash is used to punctuate clauses, not adjectives. Although not shown here, hyphens are also used to punctuate titles such as "vice-president."

COMMON SPELLING ERRORS

CORRECT THE SPELLING IN THE SENTENCE BELOW.

> The visitors will aclimate to the envirommment as soon as they become accustomed to the surroundings of the tropacs.

The words that are misspelled are "aclimate," which should be "acclimate"; "environmment," which is spelled "environment"; and "tropacs," which is spelled "tropics." It is important to learn to spell words correctly. One way to learn how to spell words is to learn how to sound out words. Break longer words down into syllables, and into affixes and roots. Get the correct spelling from a dictionary, and then practice that spelling. Practice with a few words at a time; use them in sentences. Then move on to new vocabulary words. It is also useful to remember spelling rules, such as "i before e except after c" (receive), "drop the final e" (like, liking), and "double the last consonant" when adding suffixes (stop, stopped).

SYNTAX

Syntax is the order of the words in a sentence. When writing, it is important to make sure not only that the syntax is correct, but also that it is not repetitive. There is nothing worse than reading a passage that has sentences that are all alike: noun, verb, object. These need to be interspersed with sentences that use a variety of clause constructions. This will lend a musicality to the writing, and will allow for greater flow of language and ideas. Make sure to reread any written material to ensure that the syntax is correct and engaging. Otherwise, you may end up with something that comes off as confused rather than well-written.

REWRITE THE FOLLOWING SENTENCES BY VARYING THEIR SYNTAX.

> Marilyn and Rosemary worked together. They were having a party. They had to get all the food done first. They cleaned the house and decorated. They invited about 20 people. The people were all work associates. They were having the party in Marilyn's backyard. This is where she had many similar parties. They were always fun.

THIS IS ONE WAY TO REWRITE THE SENTENCES SO THAT THE SYNTAX IS VARIED:

Marilyn and Rosemary, who worked together, were going to have a party. But before they could do that, they had to get all the food ready for it, as well as clean the house and decorate. They invited about 20 people, who were all work associates, and were holding the party in Marilyn's backyard, where there had been many other parties that were always fun.

The rewritten sentences provide a greater variety of syntax, and consequently, greater rhythm. The language is more engaging as a result. Remember to make use of clauses to introduce information and create sentences that are complex. In addition, remember to reread any work you rewrite to make sure it makes sense.

Context Clues

The term "context clues" refers to the words or phrases in the sentences that surround a new word or phrase. Context clues can often allow the reader to figure out the meaning of an unfamiliar word or phrase. Context clues may include examples of the new word or phrase, synonyms, antonyms, definitions, or contrasting information. By using context clues in the surrounding sentences, the reader can figure out approximately what the unknown word or phrase means. The placement of a word or a phrase is important, as is its function in a sentence. If a word or a phrase is being used as an adjective, the reader should look at the other adjectives in the sentence or the surrounding sentences to see if there is a clue to the word's or phrase's meaning. The location of a word or a phrase is also important. For instance, if a word or a phrase is at the beginning of a sentence, try to figure out its consequence; this may help the reader figure out its meaning.

Using context clues, determine the meaning of "fortuitous" as it is used in the following excerpt.

> Warren felt that meeting his nephew was quite fortuitous, since his nephew showed a real interest in getting involved in the company's business. Warren was hopeful that someday his nephew could take over for him.

To figure out the meaning of the word "fortuitous," the reader needs to analyze the rest of the sentence, as well as the following sentence. It would appear that their meeting was a good thing, since Warren was hopeful that his nephew could take over for him. The adjective "hopeful" helps the reader come to the conclusion that "fortuitous" means good or lucky. This is just one of the context clues. Another one would be that the nephew showed a real interest in his uncle's business. Always make sure to study the surrounding phrases and sentences for clues to an unknown word. The placement of the word or phrase and its function in the sentence are also important.

Explain how context clues can help the reader figure out the meaning of the phrase "prosthetic device" in the following excerpt.

> Modern artificial limbs are much better than artificial limbs of the past. These prosthetic devices have made it possible for amputees to run and to compete in sports. For instance, Vietnam veteran Bill Demby is able to play basketball in an aggressive, fast-paced, competitive manner thanks to high-tech plastic legs.

The placement of the phrase "prosthetic devices" helps the reader understand that the phrase is another way of saying "modern artificial limbs." This is the subject of the excerpt; the term "prosthetic devices" is a synonym for "modern artificial limbs." Even if the reader does not understand the meaning of "prosthetic," he or she can figure out the meaning of the expression. This shows how placement and context clues can assist a reader in learning the meaning of a word or an expression. Always study the information in an excerpt to better understand what is being said. The conclusion of the second sentence reinforces the meaning of the phrase by providing another synonym: "high-tech plastic legs."

How Certain Endings Can Indicate What Part of Speech a Word Is

The suffix of a word can be extremely important in telling a reader what function the word has in a sentence. Certain endings are used to make a stem an adjective; others are used to make a stem a noun. For instance, the root *consider* has many forms. It becomes a noun—*consideration*—with the addition of *-ation*. It becomes an adjective—*considerate*—with the addition of the suffix *-ate*. The adverb *considerately* can be made from the adjective *considerate* by adding *-ly*. This is a simple yet sophisticated method of figuring out what part of speech a word is.

The root word for *absolution* is *absolute*. The suffix *-tion* indicates that the word is a noun. The root could be combined with other suffixes to make other parts of speech as well. Add an *–ly* and you have the adverb *absolutely*. This word is a noun in its root form (*absolute*), so no change is needed to it. To make the verb *absolve*, the suffix *–ve* is added. This word is irregular, since most roots tend to be in verb form. It is important to be able to analyze a word, not just for its etymology, but also to determine what part of speech the word might be.

Discuss the etymology of the word fluctuate in the following sentence.

Tommy's mother noticed that his emotions tended to *fluctuate* a lot.

There really isn't a context clue in this statement, so you need to look up the word and discover its etymology to learn more about its meaning. The dictionary says that *fluctuate* is an intransitive verb, meaning it has no object. There are three syllables: fluc.tu.ate. The word has a Latin origin. It is derived from the verb "fluctuare," which means to undulate. You will also need to look up the word "undulate." It means to move in a wave-like motion, or to change continually. Synonyms of *fluctuate* are "alter," "shift," "swing," and "hesitate." In this usage, you can also see that there is a connotation of unpredictability. These clues give you a better understanding of the statement.

Using Specialized Reference Materials to Determine the Pronunciation of a Word

A print or digital dictionary can be used to find out many things about a word. A dictionary will show the correct pronunciation of a word, provide its meaning, and identify what part of speech the word is. It will also tell how the word was derived—that is, what words it came from originally. A dictionary will have a guide that shows how to sound out the words; it will use symbols to indicate sounds, and will also use sample sounds (the "a" in "bad," for instance). A dictionary lists all of the meanings of a word and the parts of speech the word can be used as. A thesaurus is useful because it lists synonyms for all the various meanings of a word, and it can help you clarify the precise meaning of a word as it is used in the text you are reading. This means you can find other words to use in a report or a text that mean the same thing as a word that may be used too often. Many books will have a glossary at the end to help you understand difficult or unfamiliar words used in the text.

Read the sentence below. Determine the meaning of "a partisan response."

While at the meeting of the homeowners' association, Jeannie had the distinct feeling that there was a partisan response when all the other tenants belligerently shouted that they were just not going to accept any more increases in maintenance assessments, no matter what the condition of the roof was.

The meaning of the phrase can be determined from the context clues in the sentence. One big clue is the fact that the "other tenants belligerently shouted..." This suggests a tone of prejudice or unreasonableness. The sentence further suggests that there was something wrong with the roof that needed repairing, and that "no matter what," the other tenants were not willing to pay. Therefore, the reader can come to the conclusion that the phrase refers to a prejudiced reaction or response. If there were not enough clues in the sentence to determine the phrase's meaning, the word "partisan" could be looked up in a dictionary. Its meaning would explain the meaning of the phrase.

Analyze the following statement by Jesus Christ, which is found in the New Testament of the Bible.

"If anyone comes to me and does not hate his own father and mother and wife and children and brothers and sisters, yes, and even his own life, he cannot be my disciple. And whoever does not carry their cross and follow me cannot be my disciple."(Luke 14:25-27)

This statement by Jesus that is quoted by Luke is an example of hyperbole. Hyperbole, or exaggeration to make a point, is frequently used throughout the Bible. It is not meant to be taken literally, and there is no command to hate family members or oneself. Rather, it is an entreaty that is meant to arouse intense emotion for maximum effect. The next sentence offers a clue in context for the reader's interpretation: one must be able to carry one's own cross (work hard) to be a disciple of Christ (i.e. to be a devout Christian). Therefore, the meaning is that devotion to God is more important than any relationship to any other family member, or any self-interest.

Nuances of "Superfluous" and "Outmoded"

Nuances are slight differences in the meanings of words that mean nearly the same thing. Nuances give words different tones or shades of meaning. They are similar to connotations, although usually more subtle. In the case of the words "superfluous" and "outmoded," superfluous conveys the sense that something is not and probably was never needed, while outmoded simply suggests that something is no longer of value since it is rendered needless due to age. Writers often use nuance to suggest something rather than saying it directly. This is often done through the choice of word or words that are used. Readers should always be aware of nuances, and should take them into account when considering the overall intent of a text.

Comprehension

It is important to acquire and accurately use words and phrases at the appropriate level to improve comprehension of various school subjects. Comprehension of academic and domain specific words is crucial to understanding the ideas and theories you will encounter as you move further in your academic career or enter the work force. Increased word knowledge that is domain specific helps individuals attain their academic and career goals. Therefore, it is very important to develop a system for increasing vocabulary through reading, using word lists, understanding word etymologies, and using new words in academic or work-related settings. A good vocabulary will result in greater personal achievements at a variety of levels.

Practice Test #1

Practice Questions

Questions 1-10 refer to the following article:

Global warming and the depletion of natural resources are constant threats to the future of our planet. All people have a responsibility to be proactive participants in the fight to save Earth by working now to conserve resources for later. Participation begins with our everyday choices. From what you buy to what you do to how much you use, your decisions affect the planet and everyone around you. Now is the time to take action.

When choosing what to buy, look for **sustainable** products made from renewable or recycled resources. The packaging of the products you buy is just as important as the products themselves. Is the item minimally packaged in a recycled container? How did the product reach the store? Locally grown food and other products manufactured within your community are the best choices. The fewer miles a product traveled to reach you, the fewer resources it required.

You can continue to make a difference for the planet in how you use what you bought and the resources you have available. Remember the locally grown food you purchased? Don't pile it on your plate at dinner. Food that remains on your plate is a wasted resource, and you can always go back for seconds. You should try to be aware of your **consumption** of water and energy. Turn off the water when you brush your teeth, and limit your showers to five minutes. Turn off the lights, and don't leave appliances or chargers plugged in when not in use.

Together, we can use less, waste less, recycle more, and make the right choices. It may be the only chance we have.

1. What is the author's primary purpose in writing this article?

a. The author's purpose is to scare people.
b. The author's purpose is to warn people.
c. The author's purpose is to inspire people.
d. The author's purpose is to inform people.

This question has two parts. Answer Part A, then answer Part B.

2. Part A: How does the author make a connection between the second and third paragraphs?

a. The author indicates he will now make suggestions for how to use what you bought.
b. The author indicates he will continue to give more examples of what you should buy.
c. The author indicates he will make suggestions for how to keep from buying more items.
d. The author indicates he will make suggestions for how to tell other people what to buy.

Part B: What specific item is used as an example in paragraph 2 and 3?

a. Water
b. Food
c. Toys
d. Driving

3. What is the main idea of this article?

a. People should use less water and energy.
b. People should make responsible choices in what they purchase and how they use their available resources.
c. People are quickly destroying the earth, and there is no way to stop the destruction.
d. People should organize everyone they know to join the fight to save the environment.

4. Which organizational pattern did the author use?

a. Comparison and contrast
b. Chronological order
c. Cause and effect
d. Problem/solution

5. What does the author say is the place to begin saving our planet?

a. The place to begin is with getting rid of products that are not earth friendly.
b. The place to begin is with using less water when we take a shower.
c. The place to begin is with the choices we make every day.
d. The place to begin is with buying locally-grown food.

This question has two parts. Answer Part A, then answer Part B.

6. Part A: What does the author imply will happen if people do not follow his suggestions?

a. The author implies we will run out of resources in the next 10 years.
b. The author implies water and energy prices will rise sharply in the near future.
c. The author implies global warming and the depletion of natural resources will continue.
d. The author implies local farmers will lose their farms.

Part B: Which sentence supports your answer from Part A?

a. Food that remains on your plate is a wasted resource, and you can always go back for seconds.
b. From what you buy to what you do to how much you use, your decisions affect the planet and everyone around you.
c. Turn off the water when you brush your teeth, and limit your showers to five minutes.
d. Global warming and the depletion of natural resources are constant threats to the future of our planet.

7. You are working with a group to compile further research on what people can do to help the environment. Your teacher has asked your group to present a broad overview of the topic. Which of the following would be the best choice for dividing the topic among the individuals in your group?

a. Products that can be recycled, products that cannot be recycled, and products that should not be recycled.
b. Products that can be recycled, products that consume less energy, and products that use recycled packaging.
c. Products that can be recycled, hybrid cars, and water conservation.
d. Products that can be recycled, products that consume less energy, and accomplishing everyday tasks using environmentally friendly practices.

8. "When choosing what to buy, look for sustainable products made from renewable or recycled resources."

What does the word "sustainable" mean in the context of this selection?

a. Able to be maintained or kept in existence
b. Produced locally
c. Chosen for specific characteristics
d. Manufactured using an energy efficient process

This question has two parts. Answer Part A, then answer Part B.

9. Part A: "You should try to be aware of your consumption of water and energy."

What does the word "consumption" mean in the context of this selection?

a. Using the greatest amount
b. Illness of the lungs
c. Using the least amount
d. Depletion of goods

Part B: Based on your answer in Part A, give a sentence from the paragraph that supports your answer.

____

____

____

10. The author makes a general suggestion to the reader: "You should try to be aware of your consumption of water and energy." Which of the following is one way the author specifies that this suggestion be carried out?

a. Food that remains on your plate is a wasted resource, and you can always go back for a second helping.
b. Locally grown food and other products manufactured within your community are the best choices.
c. Turn off the lights, and don't leave appliances or chargers plugged in when not in use.
d. Participation begins with our everyday choices.

Questions 11-19 refer to the following selection from Pride and Prejudice by Jane Austen:

It is a truth universally acknowledged, that a single man in possession of a good fortune, must be in want of a wife.

However little known the feelings or views of such a man may be on his first entering a neighbourhood, this truth is so well fixed in the minds of the surrounding families, that he is considered the rightful property of some one or other of their daughters.

"My dear Mr. Bennet," said his lady to him one day, "have you heard that Netherfield Park is let at last?"

Mr. Bennet replied that he had not.

"But it is," returned she; "for Mrs. Long has just been here, and she told me all about it."

Mr. Bennet made no answer.

"Do you not want to know who has taken it?" cried his wife impatiently.

"You want to tell me, and I have no objection to hearing it."

This was invitation enough.

"Why, my dear, you must know, Mrs. Long says that Netherfield is taken by a young man of large fortune from the north of England; that he came down on Monday in a chaise and four to see the place, and was so much delighted with it, that he agreed with Mr. Morris immediately; that he is to take possession before Michaelmas, and some of his servants are to be in the house by the end of next week."

"What is his name?"

"Bingley."

"Is he married or single?"

"Oh! Single, my dear, to be sure! A single man of large fortune; four or five thousand a year. What a fine thing for our girls!"

"How so? How can it affect them?"

"My dear Mr. Bennet," replied his wife, "how can you be so tiresome!" You must know that I am thinking of his marrying one of them."

"Is that his design in settling here?"

"Design! Nonsense, how can you talk so! But it is very likely that he may fall in love with one of them, and therefore you must visit him as soon as he comes."

"I see no occasion for that. You and the girls may go, or you may send them by themselves, which perhaps will be still better, for as you are as handsome as any of them, Mr. Bingley may like you the best of the party."

11. What is the central idea of this selection?

a. A new neighbor is due to arrive who may become good friends with Mr. and Mrs. Bennet.
b. A new neighbor is due to arrive who may be a prospective husband for one of the Bennet daughters.
c. A new neighbor is due to arrive who may be a good business connection for Mr. Bennet.
d. A new neighbor is due to arrive who has already expressed an interest in marrying one of the Bennet daughters.

12. How does Mrs. Bennet feel about the arrival of Mr. Bingley?

a. Mrs. Bennet is excited about the arrival of Mr. Bingley.
b. Mrs. Bennet is nervous about the arrival of Mr. Bingley.
c. Mrs. Bennet is afraid the arrival of Mr. Bingley will upset Mr. Bennet.
d. Mrs. Bennet is indifferent to the arrival of Mr. Bingley.

13. What does Mrs. Bennet expect from Mr. Bennet?

a. Mrs. Bennet expects Mr. Bennet to invite Mr. Bingley to a dinner party.
b. Mrs. Bennet expects Mr. Bennet to offer one of his daughters in marriage to Mr. Bingley.
c. Mrs. Bennet expects Mr. Bennet to pay a visit to Mr. Bingley.
d. Mrs. Bennet expects Mr. Bennet to invite Mr. Bingley to a ball in his honor.

14. What does Mrs. Bennet expect from Mr. Bingley?

a. Mrs. Bennet expects Mr. Bingley to be interested in marrying one of her daughters.
b. Mrs. Bennet expects Mr. Bingley to be interested in receiving a visit from Mr. Bennet.
c. Mrs. Bennet expects Mr. Bingley to love living at Netherfield Park.
d. Mrs. Bennet expects Mr. Bingley to ask for her help in choosing a wife for himself.

This question has two parts. Answer Part A, then answer Part B.

15. Part A: Which of the following statements best describes Mrs. Bennet's feelings about her husband as indicated by this selection?

a. Mrs. Bennet is tired of her husband.
b. Mrs. Bennet is exasperated by her husband.
c. Mrs. Bennet is afraid of her husband.
d. Mrs. Bennet is indifferent toward her husband.

Part B: Which sentence form the story lets you know that she feels this way?

a. Mr. Bennet thinks his wife is a great beauty.
b. "What is his name?"
c. "My dear Mr. Bennet," replied his wife, "how can you be so tiresome!"
d. "My dear Mr. Bennet," said his lady to him one day, "have you heard that Netherfield Park is let at last?"

16. This selection is set in England at the beginning of the 19th century. Drawing on information from this selection, what could you conclude was a primary goal for young women in England during this time period?

a. To marry
b. To marry a man with money
c. To entertain the neighbors
d. To be courted by as many men as possible

17. "<u>It is a truth universally acknowledged</u>, that a single man in possession of a good fortune, must be in want of a wife."

Which of the following most nearly matches the meaning of the underlined phrase?

a. Everyone knows
b. The universe has decided
c. It is a documented fact
d. It is best to tell the truth

18. "It is a truth universally acknowledged, that a single man in possession of a good fortune, must be in want of a wife."

Which of the following most nearly matches the meaning of the underlined phrase?

a. An unmarried man always wants to get married.
b. An unmarried man must want to give his money away.
c. An unmarried man with money always wants to get married.
d. An unmarried man can increase his fortune by getting married.

19. "Is that his design in settling here?"

What does the word **design** mean in the context of this selection?

a. Intention
b. Drawing
c. Creation
d. Improvisation

Questions 20 -24 pertain to the following passage:

Caged

(1) I am caged.

(2) Dim, dark, dank,

(3) Depressing metal bars

(4) Are my home,

(5) My window on the world.

(6) But for one hour each day—

(7) Sixty precious, priceless minutes—

(8) I am led from the dungeon

Into the bright, blinding light.
That is my sanctuary,
Wrapped in chain link
And barbed wire.
The air is sweeter,
Tinged with freedom
And fragranced with memories
Of a lifetime so long ago
It has almost been forgotten.
I bathe in the welcome warmth,
Cleanse my soul in the newborn breeze.
I confess my sins
In the brazen light of day,
And hope springs eternal once again.
But then they come.
My time is up.
Another hour of life has expired.
And I return to the depths
Of despair, discouragement, defeat.
Freedom, forgiveness, and faith are forgotten.
I am caged.

20. What is the connotation of the word "dungeon" in line 8?

a. The narrator lives in the basement of a castle
b. This poem is set in medieval times
c. The narrator's life is dark and unrelenting
d. The narrator is uncomfortable with life

21. What is the setting for this poem?

a. A prison
b. A farm
c. A house
d. A school

This question has two parts. Answer Part A, then answer Part B

22. Part A: Which literary device is used throughout this poem to underscore the repetitive nature of the narrator's life?

a. Simile
b. Paradox
c. Onomatopoeia
d. Alliteration

Part B: Give an example of this literary device from the story.

____

____

____

23. What point of view is used in this poem?

a. First person
b. Second person
c. Third person
d. All of the above

24. What do lines 18-22 reference?

a. The narrator's love of sunny days
b. The narrator's desire for a fresh start
c. The narrator's anger at the circumstances
d. The narrator's memories of a normal life

Questions 25– 29 pertain to the following short story:

Freedom Run

(1) The rattle of the key fumbling in the lock sent a shudder down her spine. He was home. Megan gulped down her emotions and fixed her face into a plastic smile. With a sigh, she clicked off the late show. The door swung open, and he stumbled inside.

(2) "There'sh my little Meggie-May," he crooned, slurring his words into one jumbled strand. "Howsh it goin'? What you up to tonight, little one?"

(3) He staggered toward her, arms outstretched. She stood, numb and motionless, like an observer in an overplayed scene. The same dialogue. The same motions. Rehearsed every night for some unscheduled performance. It was familiar. Too familiar.

(4) He tripped on a chair leg as he passed the dining table. The pleasant face instantly darkened as the shadow of impending rage fell. He swore loudly and turned on Megan.

(5) Why don't you clean up this pigsty," he yelled, the words clearer, colder, chilling.

(6) In two long strides, he crossed to where she still stood, rooted to the floor. She had learned long ago that backing away only prolonged the misery. His hand fell heavy across her cheek.

(7) "Lazy, good-for-nothing child," he screamed. He swore again, throwing her into the wall. "Ungrateful!"

(8) She no longer cringed as the blows landed. When he knocked her to the ground, she instinctively curled around herself, forming a tight little ball of misery. His feet crashed clumsily into her body, and she waited for it to end. In a while, it would be over. It never lasted forever.

(9) When the blows stopped, Megan struggled to her feet. She could taste the tang of blood on her split lip. She could feel the swelling in her eye. She watched him watching her. Then his face crumpled into a broken sob. He pulled her to his chest and stroked her hair.

(10) "I'm so sorry, Meggie-May. I don't mean to hurt you, darling." He sobbed louder. "Please forgive me, my little Meggie-May. I just get so mad sometimes. I won't do it again. Promise."

(11) Megan held him awkwardly, half-heartedly patting his back. "I know, Daddy," she murmured, her voice hollow. "It's okay."

(12) She led him gently to the couch and helped him sit. He clicked on the late show and settled into a subdued stupor. Megan crept upstairs and washed her battered face. She changed into a clean t-shirt and shorts and went back to the living room.

(13) "I'm going running," she announced, grabbing her house key from the table.

(14) He nodded silently. Then he glanced up. "Do me a favor before you go, Meggie-May?"

(15) "What do you need, Daddy?" she asked, knowing what he would ask for.

(16) "Bring me a beer, darling," he said with a wink.

(17) She brought him a frosty can, drowning in condensation. He took it and thanked her. Then he was lost in the eerie glow of the TV again, and Megan slipped out into the night.

(18) The cool summer breeze assaulted her senses, clearing the fog of pain and fear and anger and guilt. Her feet pattered, then pounded, then pummeled the pavement. She left the crumbling brownstone—and her crumbling life—far behind.

(19) She ran with the wind in her face and reality at her back. Running was freedom. Her aching, throbbing body loosened. Tears stung her eyes, and she submitted to the solace of sorrow. The empty streets embraced her. This was her escape.

(20) She ran for miles, past tall tenements that stretched concrete fingers toward the moon. She ran across a rust-speckled bridge, glancing down at the silent, slumbering, still depths of the river below. Across the river, larger houses sprawled on the banks. A few windows still glowed, but most were blank with darkness.

(21) It was time to go home. She knew it, even as every fiber of her body resisted. Winding her way back through silent neighborhoods, she pushed her body harder, gasping for air and aching for rest. As the streets grew darker and narrower, reality

began to close again around her heart. The freedom and release gave way to fear, and she climbed the brownstone's dirty steps.

(22) Inside, the air was stale and thick. Megan's eyes adjusted to the glare of the TV, and she saw him, sprawled on the couch. She picked up the empty beer can that dangled from his limp fingers and took it to the kitchen. When she came back, she pulled a blanket loosely over him. He stirred in his sleep, nestling into the blanket. His eyes opened halfway.

(23) "Night, Meggie-May," he murmured, turning over to face the couch.

(24) Megan turned off the TV and started up the stairs. Halfway up, she stopped and looked down. Shadows danced across his features. He looked peaceful, helpless, deceptively harmless. She loved him and hated him in one tangled surge of emotion.

(25) "Goodnight, Daddy," she whispered to the darkness. Then she turned and went upstairs.

25. What do the misspelled words in paragraph 2 indicate?

a. The author's ignorance
b. The unusual dialect
c. A misprint in the text
d. The father's intoxication

26. Which of the following paragraphs clearly indicates that the physical abuse by Megan's father is a common occurrence?

a. Paragraph 6
b. Paragraph 7
c. Paragraph 9
d. Paragraph 10

27. Why is this story set late at night in dark settings?

a. People generally drink more at night
b. Running at night is safer
c. It illustrates the darkness of Megan's life
d. The setting is coincidental

29. Why does paragraph 21 say "every fiber of her body resisted" going home?

a. She enjoyed running and wanted to run more
b. Running was a freedom from her troubled life
c. She was afraid her father might be asleep
d. The route back home was mostly uphill

29. Which paragraph best describes Megan's feelings toward her father?

a. Paragraph 11
b. Paragraph 18
c. Paragraph 21
d. Paragraph 24

Questions 30 – 34 pertain to both "Caged" and "Freedom Run":

30. What symbol of depression and trouble is used in both of these pieces?

a. Metal bars
b. Physical abuse
c. Darkness
d. Dungeons

31. What strong desire do Megan and the narrator of "Caged" have in common?

a. Strength
b. Freedom
c. Light
d. Companionship

32. Which of the following emotions best describes the state of mind of Megan and the narrator of "Caged" at the end of the passages?

a. Hopelessness
b. Confidence
c. Joy
d. Anger

33. Which of the following is the key difference between Megan and the narrator of "Caged"?

a. Megan is a female; the narrator is a male
b. Megan is young; the narrator is old
c. Megan is hopeless; the narrator is hopeful
d. Megan is a victim; the narrator is a product of choices

Short Answer Question #1

What point of view is used in these passages? How does the point of view affect the power and meaning of each of these passages? Support your answer from the texts.

Read the selection from George Washington's Farewell Address to answer questions 34-38:

The Unity of Government, which constitutes you one people, is also now dear to you.—It is justly so; for it is a main Pillar in the Edifice of your real independence; the support of your tranquility at home; your peace abroad; of your safety; of your prosperity in every shape; of that very Liberty, which you so highly prize.—But as it is easy to foresee, that, from different causes, and from different quarters, much pains will be taken, many artifices employed, to weaken in your minds the conviction of this truth;—as this is the point in your political fortress against which the batteries of internal and external enemies will be most constantly and actively (though often covertly and insidiously) directed it is of infinite moment, that you should properly estimate the immense value of your national Union to you collective and individual happiness;—that you should cherish a cordial, habitual, and immovable attachment to it; accustoming yourselves to think and speak of it as of the Palladium of your political safety and prosperity; watching for its preservation with jealous anxiety; discountenancing whatever may suggest even a suspicion, that it can in any event be abandoned, and indignantly frowning upon the first dawning of every attempt to alienate any portion of our Country from the rest, or to enfeeble the sacred ties which now link together the various parts.

For this you have every inducement of sympathy and interest.—Citizens by birth or choice of a common country, that country has a right to concentrate your affections.—The name of AMERICAN, which belongs to you, in your national capacity, must always exalt the just pride of Patriotism, more than any appellation derived from local discriminations. With slight shades of difference, you have the same Religion, Manners, Habits, and Political Principles. You have in a common cause fought and triumphed together; the Independence and Liberty you possess are the work of joint counsels, and joint efforts—of common dangers, sufferings, and successes.—

But these considerations, however powerfully they address themselves to your sensibility, are greatly outweighed by those which apply more immediately to your Interest. Here every portion of our country finds the most commanding motives for carefully guarding and preserving the Union of the whole.

34. Which of the following choices best supports the idea that Washington was concerned about the preservation of the Union?

a. "But these considerations, however powerfully they address themselves to your sensibility, are greatly outweighed by those which apply more immediately to your Interest."
b. "With slight shades of difference, you have the same Religion, Manners, Habits, and Political Principles."
c. "Here every portion of our country finds the most commanding motives for carefully guarding and preserving the Union of the whole."
d. "For this you have every inducement of sympathy and interest.—Citizens by birth or choice of a common country, that country has a right to concentrate your affections."

35. Which of the following is a key idea supported and developed in the Farewell Address?

a. The preservation of the current peace depends entirely on local actions.
b. The unity of the government is entirely at the will of the people that it governs.
c. Citizens should protect the harmony of the United States, and actively support it.
d. People who participate in discrimination of any kind are enemies of the state.

36. How does Washington connect the rights and privileges of citizens to the preservation of the Union?

a. By noting that the preservation of the Union may be under attack and that the average citizen needs to turn his attention to governing.
b. By first mentioning the value of being a citizen and then indicating that patriotism should not support discrimination .
c. By showing that this country is one that allows its citizens privileges not found in many others and that government is by the will of the people.
d. By mentioning that citizens need to keep a sharp eye on the government and develop an interest in the history of its policies.

37. What does the phrase "concentrate your affections" mean?

a. your desire for love
b. your feeling of joy
c. your deepest loyalty
d. your longing for the Union

38. What are some of the goals in this section of Washington's Farewell Speech?

a. to show that the privilege of citizenship has come at a high price and is to be valued
b. to show that citizens should be proud and need to fight foreign interests
c. to highlight the idea that the government can take over and dissolve the Union
d. to encourage citizens to value their liberties and to preserve the Union

Read the selection from Franklin Delano Roosevelt's 1941 State of the Union Address to answer questions 39- 42:

Many subjects connected with our social economy call for immediate improvement. As examples:

We should bring more citizens under the coverage of old-age pensions and unemployment insurance. We should widen the opportunities for adequate medical care. We should plan a better system by which persons deserving or needing gainful employment may obtain it.

I have called for personal sacrifice. And I am assured of the willingness of almost all Americans to respond to that call. A part of the sacrifice means the payment of more money in taxes. In my Budget Message I will recommend that a greater portion of this great defense program be paid for from taxation than we are paying for today. No person should try, or be allowed, to get rich out of the program; and the principle of tax payments in accordance with ability to pay should be constantly before our eyes to guide our legislation. If the Congress maintains these principles, the voters, putting patriotism ahead of pocketbooks, will give you their applause.

In the future days, which we seek to make secure, we look forward to a world founded upon four essential human freedoms. The first is freedom of speech and expression—everywhere in the world. The second is freedom of every person to worship God in his own way—everywhere in the world. The third is freedom from want—which, translated into world terms, means economic understandings which will secure to every nation a healthy peacetime life for its inhabitants—everywhere in the world. The fourth is freedom from fear—which, translated into world terms, means a world-wide reduction of armaments to such a point and in such a thorough fashion that no nation will be in a position to commit an act of physical aggression against any neighbor—anywhere in the world.

That is no vision of a distant millennium. It is a definite basis for a kind of world attainable in our own time and generation. That kind of world is the very antithesis of the so-called new order of tyranny which the dictators seek to create with the crash of a bomb. To that new order we oppose the greater conception—the moral order. A good society is able to face schemes of world domination and foreign revolutions alike without fear.

Since the beginning of our American history, we have been engaged in change—in a perpetual peaceful revolution—a revolution which goes on steadily, quietly adjusting itself to changing conditions—without the concentration camp or the quick-lime in the ditch. The world order which we seek is the cooperation of free countries, working together in a friendly, civilized society.

This nation has placed its destiny in the hands and heads and hearts of its millions of free men and women; and its faith in freedom under the guidance of God. Freedom means the supremacy of human rights everywhere. Our support goes to those who struggle to gain those rights and keep them. Our strength is our unity of purpose. To that high concept there can be no end save victory.

39. Which statement best supports the idea that FDR believed that America is constantly evolving toward a better situation?

a. Since the beginning of our American history, we have been engaged in change—in a perpetual peaceful revolution—a revolution which goes on steadily, quietly adjusting itself to changing conditions—without the concentration camp or the quick-lime in the ditch.
b. This nation has placed its destiny in the hands and heads and hearts of its millions of free men and women; and its faith in freedom under the guidance of God.
c. To that new order we oppose the greater conception—the moral order. A good society is able to face schemes of world domination and foreign revolutions alike without fear.
d. The fourth is freedom from fear—which, translated into world terms, means a world-wide reduction of armaments to such a point and in such a thorough fashion that no nation will be in a position to commit an act of physical aggression against any neighbor—anywhere in the world.

40. Read the following selection from a blog entry on FDR's speech. What aspect of the speech is emphasized?

> ...There is, of course, a lot to love in the speech. It highlights the important social issues of the day, the very same issues our nation is struggling with at the moment. What can we do about our elderly? Do class distinctions matter? The fact of the matter is, no one wants to take care of a sickly aging relative, regardless of class. Then again, most of our elderly don't want to live with their offspring, either—rich or poor. It begs the question...

a. It emphasizes the need for a social safety net for the aging populace.
b. It emphasizes the need for a lack of social class distinctions.
c. It highlights the fact that many of the elderly do not want long-term care.
d. It highlights the idea that people want to live independently.

41. In this text, FDR claims that raising taxes will result in a patriotic populace that will happily support the government. What might be one argument against this idea?

a. Americans are uninterested in pursuing freedom of any kind, and the four freedoms listed here are not considered important.
b. The average citizen already feels overburdened by taxes and feels the money is not being well-spent by the government.
c. Individuals will easily assent to the idea of a greater tax burden since it will naturally lead to a more prosperous state.
d. Patriots of all kinds are part of the natural makeup of America, and some will feel that the support of government is something that should be contemplated and debated.

42. What is a major theme that Roosevelt articulates in his speech?

a. It is important for all people to have access to the benefits of an old-age system that supports citizens when they can no longer work.
b. Patriotic people will feel the need to pay more taxes to the government in order to obtain certain benefits they would not be able to afford.
c. People who want to work should be able to find work without bias and without undue hardship.
d. There are four basic freedoms that are vital to the health of people: speech, worship, freedom from want, and freedom from fear.

Questions 43 – 52 pertain to the following story:

Anna Karenina

By Leo Tolstoy

(1) The young Princess Kitty Shcherbatskaya was eighteen. It was the first winter that she had been out in the world. Her success in society had been greater than that of either of her elder sisters, and greater even than her mother had anticipated. To say nothing of the young men who danced at the Moscow balls being almost all in love with Kitty, two serious suitors had already this first winter made their appearance: Levin, and immediately after his departure, Count Vronsky.

(2) Levin's appearance at the beginning of the winter, his frequent visits, and evident love for Kitty, had led to the first serious conversations between Kitty's parents as to her future, and to disputes between them. The prince was on Levin's side; he said he wished for nothing better for Kitty. The princess for her part, going round the question in the manner peculiar to women, maintained that Kitty was too young, that Levin had done nothing to prove that he had serious intentions, that Kitty felt no great attraction to him, and other side issues; but she did not state the principal point, which was that she looked for a better match for her daughter, and that Levin was not to her liking, and she did not understand him. When Levin had abruptly departed, the princess was delighted, and said to her husband triumphantly: "You see I was right." When Vronsky appeared on the scene, she was still more delighted, confirmed in her opinion that Kitty was to make not simply a good, but a brilliant match.

(3) In the mother's eyes there could be no comparison between Vronsky and Levin. She disliked in Levin his strange and uncompromising opinions and his shyness in society, founded, as she supposed, on his pride and his queer sort of life, as she considered it, absorbed in cattle and peasants. She did not very much like it that he, who was in love with her daughter, had kept coming to the house for six weeks, as though he were waiting for something, inspecting, as though he were afraid he might be doing them too great an honor by making an offer, and did not realize that a man, who continually visits at a house where there is a young unmarried girl, is bound to make his intentions clear. And suddenly, without doing so, he disappeared. "It's as well he's not attractive enough for Kitty to have fallen in love with him," thought the mother.

(4) Vronsky satisfied all the mother's desires. Very wealthy, clever, of aristocratic family, on the highroad to a brilliant career in the army and at court, and a fascinating man. Nothing better could be wished for.

(5) Vronsky openly flirted with Kitty at balls, danced with her, and came continually to the house, consequently there could be no doubt of the seriousness of his intentions. But, in spite of that, the mother had spent the whole of that winter in a state of terrible anxiety and agitation.

(6) Princess Shcherbatskaya had herself been married thirty years ago, her aunt arranging the match. Her husband, about whom everything was well known before hand, had come, looked at his future bride, and been looked at. The match-making aunt had ascertained and communicated their mutual impression. That impression had been favorable. Afterwards, on a day fixed beforehand, the expected offer was made to her parents, and accepted. All had passed very simply and easily. So it seemed, at least, to the princess. But over her own daughters she had felt how far from simple and easy is the business, apparently so commonplace, of marrying off one's daughters. The panics that had been lived through, the thoughts that had been brooded over, the money that had been wasted, and the disputes with her husband over marrying the two elder girls, Darya and Natalia! Now, since the youngest had come out, she was going through the same terrors, the same doubts, and still

more violent quarrels with her husband than she had over the elder girls. The old prince, like all fathers indeed, was exceedingly punctilious on the score of the honor and reputation of his daughters. He was irrationally jealous over his daughters, especially over Kitty, who was his favorite. At every turn he had scenes with the princess for compromising her daughter. The princess had grown accustomed to this already with her other daughters, but now she felt that there was more ground for the prince's touchiness. She saw that of late years much was changed in the manners of society, that a mother's duties had become still more difficult. She saw that girls of Kitty's age formed some sort of clubs, went to some sort of lectures, mixed freely in men's society; drove about the streets alone, many of them did not curtsey, and, what was the most important thing, all the girls were firmly convinced that to choose their husbands was their own affair, and not their parents'. "Marriages aren't made nowadays as they used to be," was thought and said by all these young girls, and even by their elders. But how marriages were made now, the princess could not learn from any one. The French fashion—of the parents arranging their children's future—was not accepted; it was condemned. The English fashion of the complete independence of girls was also not accepted, and not possible in Russian society. The Russian fashion of match-making by the offices of intermediate persons was for some reason considered unseemly; it was ridiculed by everyone, and by the princess herself. But how girls were to be married, and how parents were to marry them, no one knew. Everyone with whom the princess had chanced to discuss the matter said the same thing: "Mercy on us, it's high time in our day to cast off all that old-fashioned business. It's the young people have to marry; and not their parents; and so we ought to leave the young people to arrange it as they choose." It was very easy for anyone to say that who had no daughters, but the princess realized that in the process of getting to know each other, her daughter might fall in love, and fall in love with someone who did not care to marry her or who was quite unfit to be her husband. And, however much it was instilled into the princess that in our times young people ought to arrange their lives for themselves, she was unable to believe it, just as she would have been unable to believe that, at any time whatever, the most suitable playthings for children five years old ought to be loaded pistols. And so the princess was more uneasy over Kitty than she had been over her elder sisters.

(7) Now she was afraid that Vronsky might confine himself to simply flirting with her daughter. She saw that her daughter was in love with him, but tried to comfort herself with the thought that he was an honorable man, and would not do this. But at the same time she knew how easy it is, with the freedom of manners of today, to turn a girl's head, and how lightly men generally regard such a crime. The week before, Kitty had told her mother of a conversation she had with Vronsky during a mazurka. This conversation had partly reassured the princess; but perfectly at ease she could not be. Vronsky had told Kitty that both he and his brother were so used to obeying their mother that they never made up their minds to any important undertaking without consulting her. "And just now, I am impatiently awaiting my mother's arrival from Petersburg, as peculiarly fortunate," he told her.

(8) Kitty had repeated this without attaching any significance to the words. But her mother saw them in a different light. She knew that the old lady was expected from day to day, that she would be pleased at her son's choice, and she felt it strange that he should not make his offer through fear of vexing his mother. However, she was so anxious for the marriage itself, and still more for relief from her fears, that she believed it was so. Bitter as it was for the princess to see the unhappiness of her eldest daughter, Dolly, on the point of leaving her husband, her anxiety over the decision of her youngest daughter's fate engrossed all her feelings. Today, with Levin's reappearance, a fresh source of anxiety arose. She was afraid that her daughter, who had at one time, as she fancied, a feeling for Levin, might, from extreme sense of honor, refuse Vronsky, and that Levin's arrival might generally complicate and delay the affair so near being concluded.

(9) "Why, has he been here long?" the princess asked about Levin, as they returned home.

(10) "He came today, mamma."

(11) "There's one thing I want to say..." began the princess, and from her serious and alert face, Kitty guessed what it would be.

(12) "Mamma," she said, flushing hotly and turning quickly to her, "please, please don't say anything about that. I know, I know all about it."

(13) She wished for what her mother wished for, but the motives of her mother's wishes wounded her.

(14) "I only want to say that to raise hopes..."

(15) "Mamma, darling, for goodness' sake, don't talk about it. It's so horrible to talk about it."

(16) "I won't," said her mother, seeing the tears in her daughter's eyes; "but one thing, my love; you promised me you would have no secrets from me. You won't?"

(17) "Never, mamma, none," answered Kitty, flushing a little, and looking her mother straight in the face, "but there's no use in my telling you anything, and I...I...if I wanted to, I don't know what to say or how...I don't know..."

(18) "No, she could not tell an untruth with those eyes," thought the mother, smiling at her agitation and happiness. The princess smiled that what was taking place just now in her soul seemed to the poor child so immense and so important.

43. What is one difference between Levin and Count Vronsky?

a. Levin is shy and Count Vronsky has uncompromising opinions.
b. Levin is focused on life in the countryside while Count Vronsky has an aristocratic background.
c. Levin has uncompromising opinions while Count Vronsky is absorbed by cattle and peasants.
d. Levin is wealthy while Count Vronsky comes from an aristocratic family.

44. Read the following dictionary entry.

Fancy v. 1. To be interested in 2. To imagine something 3. To believe something that may or may not be true 4. To interpret something

Which definition best matches the way the word "fancied" is used in paragraph 8?

a. Definition 1
b. Definition 2
c. Definition 3
d. Definition 4

45. This story is set in Russia. Why is the location important to the story?

a. Princess Kitty is only interested in marrying a Russian
b. Princess Kitty will be matched according to the Russian style of using a matchmaker
c. The characters are, in part, shaped by their national heritage
d. Princess Kitty ultimately rebels against Russian society by choosing a husband using the English method

46. What is the likely importance of Vronsky's mother's arrival?

a. Vronsky is going to introduce his mother to Princess Kitty.
b. Vronsky is going to take his mother to a Moscow ball.
c. Vronsky is going to ask his mother if he should marry Kitty.
d. Vronsky is going to show his mother around Moscow.

47. In paragraph 6, the word "punctilious" most likely means:

a. careful
b. punctual
c. on time
d. jealous

48. Which sentence or phrase best demonstrates that customs in Moscow have changed?

a. The panics that had been lived through, the thoughts that had been brooded over, the money that had been wasted, and the disputes with her husband over marrying the two elder girls, Darya and Natalia!
b. She saw that girls of Kitty's age formed some sort of clubs, went to some sort of lectures, mixed freely in men's society
c. The French fashion—of the parents arranging their children's future—was not accepted
d. And so the princess was more uneasy over Kitty than she had been over her elder sisters.

49. Which sentence or phrase best illustrates why Kitty's mother thought Count Vronsky would be a good husband for Kitty?

a. When Vronsky appeared on the scene, she was still more delighted, confirmed in her opinion that Kitty was to make not simply a good, but a brilliant match.
b. She disliked in Levin his strange and uncompromising opinions and his shyness in society
c. Vronsky satisfied all the mother's desires.
d. Very wealthy, clever, or aristocratic family, on the highroad to a brilliant career in the army and at court, and a fascinating man.

50. What does the dialogue between Kitty and her mother in paragraphs 9-17 show?

a. The mother disapproves of Kitty's feelings for Levin
b. Kitty is in love with Vronsky
c. Kitty is in love with Levin
d. Kitty feels conflicted about Levin and Vronsky

This question has two parts. Answer Part A, then answer Part B

51. Part A: In paragraph 6, Kitty's mother is concerned that Kitty might marry someone who is *unfit to be her husband*. What characteristic is Kitty's mother mostly like to think makes a suitor unfit?

a. Shyness
b. A member of the aristocracy
c. Cleverness
d. Obedient

Part B: In what paragraph does Kitty's mother state this concern?

a. Paragraph 2
b. Paragraph 3
c. Paragraph 5
d. Paragraph 6

52. The author uses paragraph 1 to:

a. introduce Princess Kitty's mother
b. introduce the central conflict of the passage
c. describe the Moscow balls
d. describe Levin and Count Vronsky

Questions 53 – 60 pertain to the following passages:

Great Britain and Her Queen

By Anne E. Keeling

Chapter I

The Girl-Queen and Her Kingdom

(1) Rather more than one mortal lifetime, as we average life in these later days, has elapsed since that June morning of 1837, when Victoria of England, then a fair young princess of eighteen, was roused from her tranquil sleep in the old palace at Kensington, and bidden to rise and meet the Primate, and his dignified associates the Lord Chamberlain and the royal physician, who "were come on business of state to the Queen"—words of startling import, for they meant that, while the royal maiden lay sleeping, the aged King, whose heiress she was, had passed into the deeper sleep of death. It is already an often-told story how promptly, on receiving that summons, the young Queen rose and came to meet her first homagers, standing before them in hastily assumed wrappings, her hair hanging loosely, her feet in slippers, but in all her hearing such royally firm composure as deeply impressed those heralds of her greatness, who noticed at the same moment that her eyes were full of tears. This little scene is not only charming and touching, it is very significant, suggesting a combination of such qualities as are not always found united: sovereign good sense and readiness, blending with quick, artless feeling that sought no disguise—such feeling as again betrayed itself when on her ensuing proclamation the new Sovereign had to meet her people face to face, and stood before them at her palace window, composed but sad, the tears running unchecked down her fair pale face.

(2) That rare spectacle of simple human emotion, at a time when a selfish or thoughtless spirit would have leaped in exultation, touched the heart of England deeply, and was rightly held of happy omen. The nation's feeling is aptly expressed in the glowing verse of Mrs. Browning, praying Heaven's blessing on the "weeping Queen," and prophesying for her the love, happiness, and honour which have been hers in no stinted measure. "Thou shalt be well beloved," said the poetess; there are very few sovereigns of whom it could be so truly said that they *have* been well beloved, for not many have so well deserved it. The faith of the singer has been amply justified, as time has made manifest the rarer qualities joyfully divined in those early days in the royal child, the single darling hope of the nation.

(3) Once before in the recent annals of our land had expectations and desires equally ardent centred themselves on one young head. Much of the loyal devotion which had been alienated from the immediate family of George III had transferred itself to his grandchild, the Princess Charlotte, sole offspring of the unhappy marriage between George, Prince of Wales, and Caroline of Brunswick. The people had watched with vivid interest the young romance of Princess Charlotte's happy marriage, and had bitterly lamented her too early death—an event which had overshadowed all English hearts with forebodings of disaster. Since that dark day a little of the old attachment of England to its sovereigns had revived for the frank-mannered sailor and "patriot king," William IV; but the hopes crushed by the death of the much-regretted Charlotte had renewed themselves with even better warrant for Victoria. She was the child of no ill-omened, miserable marriage, but of a fitting union; her parents had been sundered only by death, not by wretched domestic dissensions. People heard that the mortal malady which deprived her of a father had been brought about by the Duke of Kent's simple delight in his baby princess, which kept him playing with the child when he should have been changing his wet outdoor garb; and they found something touching and tender in the tragic little circumstance. And everything that could be noticed of the manner in which the bereaved duchess was training up her precious charge spoke well for the mother's wisdom and affection, and for the future of the daughter.

(4) It was indeed a happy day for England when Edward, Duke of Kent, the fourth son of George III, was wedded to Victoria of Saxe-Coburg, the widowed Princess of Leiningen—happy, not only because of the admirable skill with which that lady conducted her illustrious child's education, and because of the pure, upright principles, the frank, noble character, which she transmitted to that child, but because the family connection established through that marriage was to be yet further serviceable to the interests of our realm. Prince Albert of Saxe-Coburg was second son of the Duchess of Kent's eldest brother, and thus first cousin of the Princess Victoria—"the Mayflower," as, in fond allusion to the month of her birth, her mother's kinsfolk loved to call her: and it has been made plain that dreams of a possible union between the two young cousins, very nearly of an age, were early cherished by the elders who loved and admired both.

(5) The Princess's life, however, was sedulously guarded from all disturbing influences. She grew up in healthy simplicity and seclusion; she was not apprised of her nearness to the throne till she was twelve years old; she had been little at Court, little in sight, but had been made familiar with her own land and its history, having received the higher education so essential to her great position; while simple truth and rigid honesty were the very atmosphere of her existence. From such a training much might be hoped; but even those who knew most and hoped most were not quite prepared for the strong individual character and power of self-determination that revealed themselves in the girlish being so suddenly transferred "from the nursery to the throne." It was quickly noticed that the part of Queen and mistress seemed native to her, and that she filled it with not more grace than propriety. "She always strikes me as possessed of singular penetration, firmness, and independence," wrote Dr. Norman Macleod in 1860; acute observers in 1837 took note of the same traits, rarer far in youth than in full maturity, and closely connected with the "reasoning, searching" quality of her mind, "anxious to get at the root and reality of things, and abhorring all shams, whether in word or deed."

(6) It was well for England that its young Sovereign could exemplify virile strength as well as womanly sweetness; for it was indeed a cloudy and dark day when she was called to her post of lonely grandeur and hard responsibility; and to fill that post rightly would have overtasked and overwhelmed a feebler nature. It is true that the peace of Europe, won at Waterloo, was still unbroken. But already, within our borders and without them, there were the signs of coming storm. The condition of Ireland was chronically bad; the condition of England was full of danger; on the Continent a new period of earth-shaking revolution announced itself not doubtfully.

(7) It would be hardly possible to exaggerate the wretched state of the sister isle, where fires of recent hate were still smouldering, and where the poor inhabitants, guilty and guiltless, were daily living on the verge of famine, over which they were soon to be driven. Their ill condition much aggravated by the intemperate habits to which despairing men so easily fall a prey. The expenditure of Ireland on proof spirits alone had in the year 1829 attained the sum of £6,000,000.

(8) In England many agricultural labourers were earning starvation wages, were living on bad and scanty food, and were housed so wretchedly that they might envy the hounds their dry and clean kennels. A dark symptom of their hungry discontent had shown itself in the strange crime of rick-burning, which went on under cloud of night season after season, despite the utmost precautions which the luckless farmers could adopt. The perpetrators were not dimly guessed to be half-famished creatures, taking a mad revenge for their wretchedness by destroying the tantalising stores of grain, too costly for their consumption; the price of wheat in the early years of Her Majesty's reign and for some time previously being very high, and reaching at one moment (1847) the extraordinary figure of a hundred and two shillings per quarter.

(9) There was threatening distress, too, in some parts of the manufacturing districts; in others a tolerably high level of wages indicated prosperity. But even in the more favoured districts there was needless suffering. The hours of work, unrestricted by law, were cruelly long; nor did there exist any restriction as to the employment of operatives of very tender years. "The cry of the children" was rising up to heaven, not from the factory only, but from the underground darkness of the mine, where a system of pitiless infant slavery prevailed, side by side with the employment of women as beasts of burden, "in an atmosphere of filth and profligacy." The condition of too many toilers was rendered more hopeless by the thriftless follies born of ignorance. The educational provision made by the piety of former ages was no longer adequate to the needs of the ever-growing nation; and all the voluntary efforts made by clergy and laity, by Churchmen and Dissenters, did not fill up the deficiency—a fact which had only just begun to meet with State recognition. It was in 1834 that Government first obtained from Parliament the grant of a small sum in aid of education. Under a defective system of poor-relief, recently reformed, an immense mass of idle pauperism had come into being; it still remained to be seen if a new Poor Law could do away with the mischief created by the old one.

(10) Looking at the earliest years of Her Majesty's rule, the first impulse is to exclaim:

(11) "And all this trouble did not pass, but grew."

53. Which of these is NOT one of the immediate problems that faced the nation at the time that Victoria was crowned?

a. Europe was not at war.
b. The people in Ireland were suffering.
c. Agricultural laborers were not earning enough money.
d. There wasn't enough money for education.

54. What is paragraph 3 mainly about?

a. Victoria's childhood
b. The royal family
c. Victoria's cousin
d. Victoria's father, the Duke of Kent

55. In paragraph 2, the author uses a quote from Mrs. Browning to show which of the following?

a. Queen Victoria was not beloved
b. Queen Victoria had a lot of happiness in her life
c. Mrs. Browning accurately predicted the people's opinion about Queen Victoria
d. Queen Victoria had a selfish and thoughtless spirit

This question has two parts. Answer Part A, then answer Part B.

56. Part A: The primary purpose of paragraphs 7-9 is to:

a. illustrate Queen Victoria's first acts as queen
b. show the poor conditions for workers in manufacturing districts
c. show the problems faced by the people of Ireland
d. describe the challenges faced by Victoria when she became queen

Part B: Give a sentence from the passage that supports your answer in Part A.

____

____

____

57. According to the author, what was one specific problem that resulted from the government's efforts to aid the poor?

a. Poverty increased
b. There wasn't enough money for education
c. The trouble grew
d. The system was reformed

58. What is one reason why Victoria's childhood was relatively simple?

a. She spent much of her childhood with her cousin
b. She didn't know she had a possibility of being queen until she was twelve
c. She was very independent
d. She received a lot of education

59. Despite the despair expressed in paragraph 11, the reader can infer which of the below?

a. Queen Victoria was not able to solve any of the problems facing the nation
b. Queen Victoria was successful in solving many of the problems facing the nation
c. The people disliked Queen Victoria's rule
d. The troubles overwhelmed Queen Victoria

60. Why is it significant that observers in 1837 noticed the same character traits in Queen Victoria as Dr. Macleod noticed in 1860?

a. Victoria had positive traits throughout her reign.
b. The traits caused problems throughout Queen Victoria's reign.
c. The traits consistently increased the anxiety of Queen Victoria's subjects.
d. The observations show that Queen Victoria's subjects were consistently displeased with her.

Answers and Explanations

1. D: Various parts of the article are intended to scare (choice A), warn (choice B), and inspire (choice C) people, but the primary purpose of the article is to offer practical advice about what products people should buy and how to use their available resources to make responsible decisions for the future of our planet.

2. Part A: A: The author begins the third paragraph with, "You can continue to make a difference for the planet in how you use what you bought and the resources you have available." This sentence makes the connection between the second paragraph which deals with what people should buy and the third paragraph which makes suggestions for how to use what they have.

Part B: B: In paragraph 2 he mentions "Locally grown food and other products," and in paragraph 3 he mentions "Remember the locally grown food you purchased?"

3. B: The author does suggest that people should use less water and energy (choice A), but these are only two suggestions among many and not the main idea of the article. The article does not say that people are destroying the earth (choice C) or make a suggestion that people organize their acquaintances (choice D).

4. D: The author presents the problems of global warming and the rapid depletion of the planet's natural resources and offers several practical suggestions for how to stop global warming and use remaining resources judiciously.

5. C: The author makes suggestions to use less water (choice B) and buy locally grown food (choice D), but they are not suggested as the place to begin saving the planet. The author does not suggest getting rid of products that are not earth friendly (choice A). The author states: "Participation begins with our everyday choices."

6. Part A: C: The author does not mention running out of resources in a specific time period (choice A), the cost of water and energy (choice B), or the possibility of hardship for local farmers (choice D).

Part B: D: The sentence that best shows that the author is implying that global warming and the depletion of natural resources will continue is, "Global warming and the depletion of natural resources are constant threats to the future of our planet."

7. D: Choice D gives the broadest interpretation of the topic. Choice A focuses solely on recycling; choice B focuses on the choice of products to be purchased; and choice C focuses on recycling, one type of energy-saving product (hybrid cars), and ways to conserve one resource (water).

8. A: "When choosing what to buy, look for sustainable products made from renewable or recycled resources." The context of this sentence indicates that sustainable means renewable or able to be used again.

9. Part A: D: As the passage states: "You should try to be aware of your consumption of water and energy. Turn off the water when you brush your teeth, and limit your showers to five minutes. Turn off the lights, and don't leave appliances or chargers plugged in when not in use." The contexts of these sentences indicate that consumption means the depletion of goods (e.g., water and energy).

Part B: Any of the sentences above that give context to what the word "consumption" mean are acceptable answers.

10. C: Of the choices available, this is the only sentence that offers specific ideas for carrying out the author's suggestion to the reader of limiting consumption of energy.

11. B: There is no indication in the passage that the Bennets are interested in becoming friends with Mr. Bingley (choice A), that Mr. Bingley would be a valuable business connection (choice C), or that Mr. Bingley has any prior knowledge of the Bennet daughters (choice D). Mrs. Bennet tells her husband that a new neighbor is moving in: "Mrs. Long says that Netherfield is taken by a young man of large fortune." Mrs. Bennet is sure he will make an excellent husband for one of her daughters: "You must know that I am thinking of his marrying one of them."

12. A: Mrs. Bennet feels that Mr. Bingley is likely to marry one of her daughters. She tells her husband that Mr. Bingley is a "single man of large fortune; four or five thousand a year. What a fine thing for our girls!"

13. C: Mrs. Bennet wants her husband to be acquainted with Mr. Bingley so that he can introduce Mr. Bingley to their daughters: "But it is very likely that he may fall in love with one of them, and therefore you must visit him as soon as he comes."

14. A: Mrs. Bennet remarks to her husband, "But it is very likely that he may fall in love with one of them, and therefore you must visit him as soon as he comes."

15. Part A: B: Mrs. Bennet is exasperated by her husband, meaning that she is frustrated or annoyed and fed up with her husband's seeming indifference to Mr. Bingley: "'My dear Mr. Bennet,' replied his wife, 'how can you be so tiresome!'" Being annoyed would indicate that she is not indifferent toward him. She also is the person who initiated the dialog and seems to eagerly want to talk to him about her ideas. This would indicate that she is neither tired nor afraid of her husband.

Part B: C: This sentence best represents how she feels about her husband.

16. B: The evidence in this selection indicates that marrying a man with money was a primary goal for young women. Mrs. Bennet tells Mr. Bennet that Mr. Bingley is "A single man of large fortune; four or five thousand a year." Mrs. Bennet further indicates that she is thrilled with the news because of Mr. Bingley's potential as a husband for one of her daughters: "What a fine thing for our girls... You must know that I am thinking of his marrying one of them."

17. A: "It is a truth universally acknowledged" means that something is understood to be true by the general public.

18. C: "A single man in possession of a good fortune, must be in want of a wife" means that if a man has enough money to support a wife in comfort, he must want to find a wife as soon as possible.

19. A: Mr. Bennet is facetiously asking if the idea of marriage (particularly to one of his own daughters) was Mr. Bingley's intention when he agreed to rent Netherfield Park.

20. C: is the best choice because the connotation of the word "dungeon" is that the narrator's life is dark and unrelenting. A, B, and D are not the best choices because they do not accurately represent the real connotation of the word "dungeon."

21. A: is the best choice because "Caged" is set in a prison, as can be deduced from careful reading. B, C, and D are not the best choices because the poem is not set on a farm or in a house or school.

22. Part A: D: is the best choice because alliteration is used throughout the poem to underscore the repetitive nature of the narrator's life. A, B, and C are not the best choices because simile, paradox, and onomatopoeia are not used throughout this poem.

Part B: There are several examples that can be used here. Two of them are, "Dim, dark, dank" and "bright, blinding light".

23. A: is the best choice because this poem is written using first-person point of view.

24. B: is the best choice because lines 18-22 reference the narrator's desire for a fresh start.

25. D: is the best choice because the misspelled words in paragraph 2 indicate slurred speech caused by the father's intoxication.

26. A: is the best choice because paragraph 6 clearly shows that the physical abuse by Megan's father is a common occurrence.

27. C: is the best choice because "Freedom Run" is set late at night in dark settings to illustrate the darkness that parental abuse creates in Megan's life.

28. B: is the best choice because paragraph 21 is meant to indicate that Megan did not want to go home because running represents freedom from her troubled life.

29. D: is the best choice because paragraph 24 is the portion of the story that best describes Megan's feelings toward her father.

30. C: is the best choice because darkness is the symbol of depression and trouble that is used in both pieces.

31. B: is the best choice because Megan and the narrator of "Caged" both strongly desire freedom.

32. A: is the best choice because, at the end of both pieces, both Megan and the narrator of "Caged" demonstrate a sense of hopelessness.

33. D: is the best choice because the key difference between Megan and the narrator of "Caged" is that Megan is a victim, while the narrator is a product of choices.

Sample Short Answer #1

> "Caged" is written in first-person point of view. This gives the reader an inside perspective on what the narrator is thinking and feeling. With the use of the first-person pronoun "I," the reader feels intimately connected to the narrator, increasing the power of the passage.
>
> In contrast to "Caged," "Freedom Run" is written in third-person point of view. This gives the reader a broad perspective on Megan's life and her situation. It also allows the author to include details that could not be included in first-person writing. This increases the power of the writing by making it more objective.

34. C: "Here every portion of our country finds the most commanding motives for carefully guarding and preserving the Union of the whole."

This sentence clearly indicates that the Union may be under some sort of threat: Washington uses the word *guarding*, showing that there was the possibility of attack. The other choices contribute to Washington's theme, but they do not clearly illustrate the uneasiness found in this sentence.

35. C: Citizens should protect the harmony of the United States, and actively support it.

This part of the speech addresses Washington's concern over the unity of the nation. He indicates that the privileges enjoyed by citizens should not be taken for granted. Choices A and B do not address the main theme of this selection. Choice D is a distortion of one of Washington's ideas.

36. B: By first mentioning the value of being a citizen and then indicating that patriotism should not support discrimination.

Washington unpacks his points by first noting the privilege of being a citizen and then mentioning that discrimination can be a possible obstacle to preserving the Union. The other choices mention ideas that are found in the passage, but they are not part of the connection between the rights of citizens and the preservation of the budding nation.

37. C: your deepest loyalty

Washington wrote in a style not typically utilized today. From the context of the surrounding sentences, it is clear that he is hoping that regular people turn their hearts toward their country and have the highest regard for it. The other choices focus more on the individual's feelings for himself.

38. D: to encourage citizens to value their liberties and to preserve the Union

This is the focus of this selection. Choice A only mentions one goal. Choices B and C are taken from some of the details in the passage.

39. A: Since the beginning of our American history, we have been engaged in change—in a perpetual peaceful revolution—a revolution which goes on steadily, quietly adjusting itself to changing conditions—without the concentration camp or the quick-lime in the ditch.

This is the only statement listed here that directly supports the idea that FDR thought that America is constantly moving toward a better way of life.

40. A: It emphasizes the need for a social safety net for the aging populace.

While the other ideas in Choices B and C are clearly mentioned in the blog, they are not derived from the speech. Choice A is the only one that discusses an idea that shows up in the speech.

41. B: The average citizen already feels overburdened by taxes and feels the money is not being well-spent by the government.

The argument that needs to be evaluated is that people will be happy to give more money in taxes to the government. It would be safe to raise the counterargument that the general population may already believe they are paying enough in taxes and don't think the government is spending that money wisely. Not everyone will be happy to give more to the government to spend. Choices A and D do not address the question. Choice C actually agrees with FDR's premise.

42. D: There are four basic freedoms that are vital to the health of people: speech, worship, freedom from want, and freedom from fear.

This speech is typically referred to as the "Four Freedoms" speech. In it, FDR articulates the basic freedoms he believes in. These freedoms are the central focus of the speech, since it supports the other ideas that he is focusing on (ie, social issues). Choice A is a detail in the speech, Choice B is not articulated, and Choice C is not in the speech.

43. B: because the passage says in paragraph 3 that Levin is absorbed in cattle and peasants, which can be found in the countryside. Paragraph 4 states that Vronsky comes from an aristocratic background, or family. While it's true that Levin is shy, choice A is incorrect because Levin is the character who has uncompromising opinions, not Vronsky. Choice C is incorrect because it is Levin who is absorbed by cattle and peasants, not Vronsky. Choice D is incorrect because paragraph 4 states that Vronsky is wealthy, not Levin.

44. C: because the context of the sentence shows that Kitty's mother believed, or fancied, that Kitty had feelings for Levin. While it might also be true that Kitty fancies (or is interested in Levin), choice A is incorrect because the structure of the sentence shows that *fancied* is used to show the mother's opinion. Choice C is incorrect because Kitty's mother is not imagining Kitty's feelings; based on Kitty's behavior earlier, she believes that Kitty was in love with Levin. Choice D is incorrect because Kitty's mother is not interpreting current events; instead, she fancies that Kitty had feelings for Levin based on her observations of Kitty's past behavior.

45. C: is the correct answer because Kitty's mother is torn by the changes that are reshaping her society. The reader can best understand the impact of these changes by understanding original Russian society, which is partly explained in paragraphs 1 and 6. Choice A is incorrect because the passage does not present evidence that Kitty is only interested in marrying a Russian; while this may be true, the passage does not indicate Kitty's feelings. Choice B is incorrect because paragraph 6 states that the Russian style of matchmaking was unseemly and no longer used. Choice D is incorrect because the reader does not yet know whom Kitty will marry or whether Kitty will use the English method by choosing her husband herself.

46. C: that Vronsky is going to ask his mother if he should marry Kitty. Paragraph 7 says that Vronsky never makes important decisions without consulting his mother, and her visit will be an opportunity for him to ask her important questions. Choice A is incorrect because the passage doesn't indicate that Kitty might meet Vronsky's mother. Choice B is incorrect because Vronsky attends balls to dance with Kitty, not his mother. While Vronsky might show his mother around Moscow, choice D is incorrect because the passage does not imply that this will happen.

47. A: because the rest of the sentence explains that Kitty's father is punctilious about his daughters' honor and reputation, which means that he's careful to guard them. Choice B is incorrect because *punctual* means to be on time, and the passage doesn't show Kitty's father attempting to arrive anywhere promptly. Choice C is incorrect because it has the same meaning as punctual. Choice D is incorrect because *jealous* is used in the following sentence and is used to show that he guards his daughters carefully.

48. B: because it gives specific details about new behaviors, such as forming clubs and going to lectures. Choice A is incorrect because it focuses on the stress Kitty's mother felt as Kitty's older daughters got married. Choice C is incorrect because it shows that the French fashion was not accepted; this means that Russian society has not changed to embrace the French fashion. Choice D is incorrect because it shows Kitty's mother is increasingly uneasy but does not show why.

49. D: because this answer shows the specific attributes that Kitty's mother likes about Vronsky, such as wealth and cleverness. Choice A is incorrect because it only states that Kitty's mother likes

Vronsky; however, this choice does not explain why. Choice B is incorrect because it shows that Kitty's mother dislikes Levin without explaining why she likes Vronsky. Choice C is incorrect because it simply states that Kitty's mother likes Vronsky.

50. D: is the correct answer because Kitty shows her inner conflict without even mentioning Levin or Vronsky's names. However, Kitty clearly shows her distress, such as when she cries in paragraph 16 and says, "It's so horrible," in paragraph 15. Choice A is incorrect because the mother doesn't express her opinion during the dialogue; instead, she's simply trying to understand how Kitty's feeling. Choices B and C are incorrect because Kitty doesn't express her feelings for either Levin or Vronsky; at this point in the story, she is very conflicted.

51. Part A: because paragraph 3 says that Kitty's mother dislikes Levin's shyness. Choices B and C are incorrect because these are the characteristics mentioned in paragraph 4 as positive traits that Vronsky has. Even though Vronsky, the mother's favorite, is very obedient to his mother, Kitty's mother does say that this trait makes him unsuitable for Kitty. She is a little uneasy about this trait, but does not rule Vronsky out as an acceptable husband. Therefore, choice D is incorrect.

Part B: B: In paragraph 3, Kitty's mother says that she dislikes Levin's shyness.

52. B: because the paragraph shows that the central conflict is Kitty's feelings about Levin and Vronsky. Choice A is incorrect because Kitty's mother does not appear prominently in paragraph 1. Choice C is incorrect because the paragraph only mentions the balls but does not give any details. Choice D is incorrect because the reader only learns details about Levin and Vronsky in the following paragraphs, not in paragraph 1.

53. A: because paragraph 6 explains that the peace that came upon Europe after the battle of Waterloo was still unbroken; the continent was not at war. Choices B, C, and D are incorrect because paragraphs 7-9 explain that these choices were problems. Paragraph 7 talks about the problems in Ireland, paragraph 8 talks about the low, or starvation, wages earned by many agricultural workers, and paragraph 9 mentions the problems with the education system.

54. B: because the paragraph talks primarily about the royal family, including George III and Princess Charlotte. This paragraph serves to partially explain how Victoria came to be queen. Choice A is incorrect because the paragraph gives few details about Victoria's childhood. Instead, it talks about her father and other royals. Choice C is incorrect because paragraph 4, not paragraph 3, talks about Albert, Victoria's cousin. Choice D is incorrect because only a portion of the paragraph discusses the Duke of Kent. The paragraph is mainly about the royal family as a whole.

55. C: is the correct answer because the paragraph shows that Mrs. Browning predicted that the people would love Victoria and that the people did, ultimately, love her (the paragraph says "there are very few sovereigns of whom it could be so truly said that they *have* been well beloved"). Choice A is incorrect because it is the opposite of how the people felt about her. Choice B is incorrect because the quote does not mention any poets other than Mrs. Browning. Choice D is incorrect because the passage does not state that Queen Victoria had those characteristics.

56. Part A: D: is the correct answer because the paragraphs give many details about the troubles that faced the nation when Victoria became queen. Choice A is incorrect because they don't describe what Queen Victoria did to address these problems. Choices B and C are incorrect because the paragraphs discuss many problems, not just those specific problems.

Part B: Any sentence that showed some of the troubles that the nation was facing when Queen Victoria took over would be correct. Example sentence: In England many agricultural labourers were earning starvation wages, were living on bad and scanty food, and were housed so wretchedly that they might envy the hounds their dry and clean kennels.

57. A: because paragraph 9 states that the system of poor-relief was defective, leading to an immense amount of poverty. Choice B is incorrect because the lack of funding for education is presented as a separate problem from the efforts to aid the poor. Choice C is incorrect because it is not specific and could apply to many of the problems described in paragraphs 7-9. Choice D is incorrect because the government had already reformed the poor-relief system in a failed attempt to solve the problems, and we have not yet seen whether new reforms are coming.

58. B: because paragraph 5 says that Victoria did not know how close she was to the throne until she was twelve years old. This supports the author's point earlier in the sentence that her childhood was simple. Choice A is incorrect because the passage never says she spent time with her cousin; instead, paragraph 4 simply describes Prince Albert's lineage. Choice C is incorrect because the author does not indicate that Victoria's independence is related to her simplicity. Choice D is incorrect because the passage does not imply that the education caused her childhood to be simple. Instead, the education prepared her for the throne.

59. B: because the reader knows from paragraph 2 that Queen Victoria was beloved. The reader can infer that she would not have been beloved if she had been unable to improve life for her subjects. Choice A is incorrect due to the reader's assumption from paragraph 2 that Victoria solved some of the problems was therefore well-loved by the people. Choice C is incorrect because the reader can infer that Victoria faced many challenges, but the reader already knows that people liked her rule. Choice D is incorrect because the high-regard with which the people gave Queen Victoria shows that the troubles likely didn't overwhelm her.

60. A: because the traits described by Dr. Macleod are positive traits that contributed to the queen's strengths. Since they were observed both in 1837 and 1860, the reader can infer that the queen had these traits throughout her reign. Choice B is incorrect because the traits described are positive; the passage does not indicate that they caused problems. Choice C is incorrect because Dr. Macleod and the other observers seem to admire these traits, which means they did not cause anxiety. Choice D is incorrect because the traits are positive traits, which means that Queen Victoria's subjects were unlikely to be displeased.

Practice Test #2

Practice Questions

Questions 1-10 refer to the following passage:

Helen Keller was born on June 27, 1880. She was a happy and healthy child until the age of 19 months when she fell ill with a terrible fever. Although Helen recovered from the fever, it left her both deaf and blind.

Helen was loved and cared for by her doting parents, but her behavior became erratic after she lost her hearing and sight, with unpredictable outbursts of temper. Her parents were at a loss how to reach her and teach her how to behave. Helen herself was frustrated and lonely in her dark, silent world. All of that began to change in March 1887 when Anne Sullivan came to live with the Kellers and be Helen's teacher.

Anne taught Helen to communicate by forming letters with her fingers held in another person's hand. In this way, Teacher, as Helen called her, taught her pupil to spell cake, doll, and milk. However, it was not until Anne spelled w-a-t-e-r in Helen's hands as cold water gushed over both of them that Helen made the exciting connection between the words and the world around her. This connection engendered an insatiable curiosity within Helen. After that day, Helen learned at an incredible rate with Teacher by her side.

Helen went on to graduate from Radcliffe College. She became a famous writer, speaker, and advocate. The story of Helen's remarkable life is known worldwide. Anne Sullivan and Helen Keller were inseparable until Anne's death in 1936. Teacher shined a light in Helen's dark world and showed her the way.

1. Which organizational pattern does the author use?

a. Comparison and contrast
b. Chronological order
c. Cause and effect
d. Problem/solution

2. Which of the following would make the best topic sentence for this passage?

a. Helen Keller, with the untiring help of her teacher Anne Sullivan, became a shining example of how to rise above disabilities.
b. Anne Sullivan helped Helen Keller break free from the dark silence inflicted by a childhood fever.
c. Helen Keller and Anne Sullivan were the greatest of friends.
d. Helen Keller was a brave woman who overcame many obstacles on her road to success.

3. What is the author's primary purpose in writing this passage?

a. To inform people about Helen Keller's college career
b. To inform people about Anne Sullivan's life
c. To inform people about services available for the deaf and blind
d. To inform people about Helen Keller's life

4. How does the author make a connection between the second and third paragraphs?

a. The author begins the third paragraph by continuing to talk about Helen's parents who were introduced in the second paragraph.
b. The author organizes the second and third paragraphs the same way.
c. The author ends the second paragraph with the advent of Anne Sullivan in Helen's life, and begins the third paragraph with the most important contribution Anne made to Helen's education.
d. The author uses the third paragraph to elaborate on Helen's frustration and resulting temper tantrums introduced in the second paragraph.

5. What is the author's tone in this passage?

a. Indifferent
b. Censorious
c. Admiring
d. Impartial

6. Part A: Why was Helen frustrated as a child?

a. Helen was frustrated that her parents could not teach her to communicate.
b. Helen was frustrated that she couldn't communicate with other people.
c. Helen was frustrated that Anne came to live with the Kellers.
d. Helen was frustrated that she was unable to make the connection between the words cake, doll, and milk and the objects they represent.

Part B: How did she react to the frustration?

a. She just sat back and dealt with it.
b. She would tell Anne to come help her
c. She would have unpredictable outbursts of temper
d. She would play with her dolls

7. What was the turning point in Helen's life?

a. When Helen learned to connect feeling water on her hands with the word "water."
b. When Helen graduated from Radcliffe College.
c. When Helen contracted the fever that took away her hearing and sight.
d. When Anne Sullivan came to live with the Kellers and be Helen's teacher.

8. Which of the following can you infer was true about Helen's parents?

a. Helen's parents were frustrated that they were unable to help Helen communicate.
b. Helen's parents were jealous that Anne Sullivan was closer to Helen than they were.
c. Helen's parents were glad to give Anne Sullivan full responsibility for Helen.
d. Helen's parents wanted their daughter to graduate from Radcliffe College.

9. What does the word "engendered" mean as it is used in this sentence?

This connection engendered an insatiable curiosity within Helen.

a. Caused to exist
b. Made sense of
c. Connected
d. Satisfied

10. What does the word "insatiable" mean as it is used in this sentence?

This connection engendered an insatiable curiosity within Helen.

a. Unbelievable
b. Indestructible
c. Unsatisfiable
d. Indescribable

Questions 11-15 refer to the following passage:

In the United States, the foreign language requirement for high school graduation is decided at the state level. This means the requirement varies, with some states deciding to forego a foreign language requirement altogether (www.ncssfl.org). It is necessary that these states reconsider their position and amend their requirements to reflect compulsory completion of a course of one or more foreign languages. Studying a foreign language has become increasingly important for the global economy. As technology continues to make international business relations increasingly easy, people need to keep up by increasing their communication capabilities. High school graduates with foreign language credits have been shown to have an increased college acceptance rate. In addition, students who have mastered more than one language typically find themselves in greater demand when they reach the job market. Students who did not study a foreign language often find themselves unable to obtain a job at all.

11. What is the main idea of this passage?

a. Studying a foreign language will help graduating students find jobs after high school.
b. Studying a foreign language should be a mandatory requirement for high school graduation.
c. Studying a foreign language helps students gain an understanding of other cultures.
d. Studying a foreign language is essential if a student hopes to get into college.

12. Which of the following statements represents the best summary of the claims made in this passage?

a. Studying a foreign language is important if you want to graduate from high school and get a job.
b. Studying a foreign language is important for the global economy because of the technological advances that have been made in international communications.
c. Studying a foreign language is important for the global economy, college acceptance rates, and becoming a sought-after candidate in the job market.
d. Studying a foreign language is important for college acceptance rates and obtaining a job after college.

13. Which of the following statements represents an EXAGGERATED claim in support of the argument presented in this passage?

a. In the United States, the foreign language requirement for high school graduation is decided at the state level.
b. Studying a foreign language has become increasingly important for the global economy.
c. High school graduates with foreign language credits have been shown to have an increased college acceptance rate.
d. Students who did not study a foreign language often find themselves unable to obtain a job at all.

14. Which of the following would be a useful source of information to determine the validity of the argument presented in this passage?

a. A survey of high school students' preferences with regard to foreign language requirements
b. A comparison of the correlation between a second language introduced at home and subsequent college acceptance rates
c. A survey that asks parents to select the foreign language they would like their children to study in high school
d. A comparison of the correlation between high school students' study of a foreign language and subsequent college acceptance rates

15. Which of the following would be the best concluding statement for this passage?

a. States should consider how important foreign languages are for the global economy when making their policies regarding foreign language requirements for graduation from high school.
b. Policies regarding a foreign language requirement for graduation from high school should take into account the importance of foreign languages for the global economy and the correlation between foreign languages and increased college acceptance rates and employment opportunities.
c. High school graduation requirements should include a foreign language class because of the influence knowledge of a second language has on college acceptance rates.
d. Policies regarding a foreign language requirement for graduation from high school should take into account how difficult it is to obtain a job in today's economy for those who do not have knowledge of more than one language.

Questions 16-21 refer to the following selection from Little Women by Louisa May Alcott:

"Christmas won't be Christmas without any presents," grumbled Jo, lying on the rug.

"It's so dreadful to be poor!" sighed Meg, looking down at her old dress.

"I don't think it's fair for some girls to have plenty of pretty things, and other girls nothing at all," added little Amy, with an injured sniff.

"We've got Father and Mother, and each other," said Beth contentedly from her corner.

The four young faces on which the firelight shone brightened at the cheerful words, but darkened again as Jo said sadly, "We haven't got Father, and shall not have him for a long time." She didn't say "perhaps never," but each silently added it, thinking of Father far away, where the fighting was.

Nobody spoke for a minute; then Meg said in an altered tone, "You know the reason Mother proposed not having any presents this Christmas was because it is going to be a hard winter for everyone; and she thinks we ought not to spend money for pleasure, when our men are suffering so in the army. We can't do much, but we can make our little sacrifices, and ought to do it gladly. But I am afraid I don't," and Meg shook her head, as she thought regretfully of all the pretty things she wanted.

"But I don't think the little we should spend would do any good. We've each got a dollar, and the army wouldn't be much helped by our giving that. I agree not to expect anything from Mother or you, but I do want to buy Undine and Sintran for myself. I've wanted it so long," said Jo, who was a bookworm.

"I planned to spend mine in new music," said Beth, with a little sigh, which no one heard but the hearth brush and kettle-holder.

"I shall get a nice box of Faber's drawing pencils; I really need them," said Amy decidedly.

"Mother didn't say anything about our money, and she won't wish us to give up everything. Let's each buy what we want, and have a little fun; I'm sure we work hard enough to earn it," cried Jo, examining the heels of her shoes in a gentlemanly manner.

"I know I do—teaching those tiresome children nearly all day, when I'm longing to enjoy myself at home," began Meg, in the complaining tone again.

"You don't have half such a hard time as I do," said Jo. "How would you like to be shut up for hours with a nervous, fussy old lady, who keeps you trotting, is never satisfied, and worries you till you're ready to fly out the window or cry?"

"It's naughty to fret, but I do think washing dishes and keeping things tidy is the worst work in the world. It makes me cross, and my hands get so stiff, I can't practice well at all." And Beth looked at her rough hands with a sigh that anyone could hear that time.

"I don't believe any of you suffer as I do," cried Amy, "for you don't have to go to school with impertinent girls, who plague you if you don't know your lessons, and laugh at your dresses, and label your father if he isn't rich, and insult you when your nose isn't nice."

"If you mean libel, I'd say so, and not talk about labels, as if Papa was a pickle bottle," advised Jo, laughing.

16. Which of the following sentences best describes the theme of this passage?

a. You should always use the biggest words you know.
b. The youngest member of a family should do the most work.
c. Everyone has problems, and it is important to think of others.
d. You should spend your money on yourself because you deserve it.

17. Which choice gives the best summary of the problems presented in this passage?

a. Father is away at war, money is scarce, and the sisters are unhappy with their responsibilities.
b. Mother forbade any presents this Christmas, and the sisters are unhappy with their responsibilities.
c. The sisters do not have as much money to spend as they would like, and Amy is made fun of at school.
d. Beth is tired of cleaning and washing dishes, and Father is away at war.

18. What do you know to be true about Father?

a. He wants the sisters to spend their money on themselves.
b. He misses his wife and children.
c. He wants the sisters to give their money to the army.
d. He is with the army.

19. What do you know to be true about Mother?

a. She misses her husband.
b. She is sorry that the family is poor.
c. She proposed not having presents.
d. She wants the sisters to spend their money on themselves.

20. Who is the only sister who does NOT specify what she wants to buy with her money?

a. Amy
b. Beth
c. Jo
d. Meg

21. What does the phrase "no one heard but the hearth brush and kettle holder" tell the reader about where Beth is located in the room?

> "I planned to spend mine in new music," said Beth, with a little sigh, which no one heard but the hearth brush and kettle-holder.

a. Near the stove
b. By the window
c. In the kitchen
d. Closest to the fireplace

Questions 22 – 31 pertain to the following story:

Roughing It by Mark Twain, Part 1

Chapter I

(1) My brother had just been appointed Secretary of Nevada Territory—an office of such majesty that it concentrated in itself the duties and dignities of Treasurer, Comptroller, Secretary of State, and Acting Governor in the Governor's absence. A salary of eighteen hundred dollars a year and the title of "Mr. Secretary," gave to the great position an air of wild and imposing grandeur. I was young and ignorant, and I envied my brother. I coveted his distinction and his financial splendor, but particularly and especially the long, strange journey he was going to make, and the curious new world he was going to explore. He was going to travel! I never had been away from home, and that word "travel" had a seductive charm for me. Pretty soon he would be hundreds and hundreds of miles away on the great plains and deserts, and among the mountains of the Far West, and would see buffaloes and Indians, and prairie dogs, and antelopes, and have all kinds of adventures, and may be get hanged or scalped, and have ever such a fine time, and write home and tell us all about it, and be a hero. And he would see the gold mines and the silver mines, and maybe go about of an afternoon when his work was done, and pick up two or three pailfuls of shining slugs, and nuggets of gold and silver on the hillside. And by and by he would become very rich, and return home by sea, and be able to talk as calmly about San Francisco

and the ocean, and "the isthmus" as if it was nothing of any consequence to have seen those marvels face to face.

(2) What I suffered in contemplating his happiness, pen cannot describe. And so, when he offered me, in cold blood, the sublime position of private secretary under him, it appeared to me that the heavens and the earth passed away, and the firmament was rolled together as a scroll! I had nothing more to desire. My contentment was complete.

(3) At the end of an hour or two I was ready for the journey. Not much packing up was necessary, because we were going in the overland stage from the Missouri frontier to Nevada, and passengers were only allowed a small quantity of baggage apiece. There was no Pacific railroad in those fine times of ten or twelve years ago—not a single rail of it. I only proposed to stay in Nevada three months—I had no thought of staying longer than that. I meant to see all I could that was new and strange, and then hurry home to business. I little thought that I would not see the end of that three-month pleasure excursion for six or seven uncommonly long years!

(4) I dreamed all night about Indians, deserts, and silver bars, and in due time, next day, we took shipping at the St. Louis wharf on board a steamboat bound up the Missouri River.

(5) We were six days going from St. Louis to "St. Jo."—a trip that was so dull, and sleepy, and eventless that it has left no more impression on my memory than if its duration had been six minutes instead of that many days. No record is left in my mind, now, concerning it, but a confused jumble of savage-looking snags, which we deliberately walked over with one wheel or the other; and of reefs which we butted and butted, and then retired from and climbed over in some softer place; and of sand-bars which we roosted on occasionally, and rested, and then got out our crutches and sparred over.

(6) In fact, the boat might almost as well have gone to St. Jo. by land, for she was walking most of the time, anyhow—climbing over reefs and clambering over snags patiently and laboriously all day long. The captain said she was a "bully" boat, and all she wanted was more "shear" and a bigger wheel. I thought she wanted a pair of stilts, but I had the deep sagacity not to say so.

Chapter II

(7) The first thing we did on that glad evening that landed us at St. Joseph was to hunt up the stage-office, and pay a hundred and fifty dollars apiece for tickets per overland coach to Carson City, Nevada.

(8) The next morning, bright and early, we took a hasty breakfast, and hurried to the starting-place. Then an inconvenience presented itself which we had not properly appreciated before, namely, that one cannot make a heavy traveling trunk stand for twenty-five pounds of baggage—because it weighs a good deal more. But that was all we could take—twenty-five pounds each. So we had to snatch our trunks open, and make a selection in a good deal of a hurry. We put our lawful twenty-five pounds apiece all in one valise, and shipped the trunks back to St. Louis again. It was a sad parting, for now we had no swallow-tail coats and white kid gloves to wear at Pawnee receptions in the Rocky Mountains, and no stove-pipe hats nor patent-leather boots,

nor anything else necessary to make life calm and peaceful. We were reduced to a war-footing. Each of us put on a rough, heavy suit of clothing, woolen army shirt and "stogy" boots included; and into the valise we crowded a few white shirts, some under-clothing and such things. My brother, the Secretary, took along about four pounds of United States statutes and six pounds of Unabridged Dictionary; for we did not know—poor innocents—that such things could be bought in San Francisco on one day and received in Carson City the next. I was armed to the teeth with a pitiful little Smith & Wesson's seven-shooter, which carried a ball like a homoeopathic pill, and it took the whole seven to make a dose for an adult. But I thought it was grand. It appeared to me to be a dangerous weapon. It only had one fault—you could not hit anything with it. One of our "conductors" practiced awhile on a cow with it, and as long as she stood still and behaved herself she was safe; but as soon as she went to moving about, and he got to shooting at other things, she came to grief. The Secretary had a small-sized Colt's revolver strapped around him for protection against the Indians, and to guard against accidents he carried it uncapped. Mr. George Bemis was dismally formidable. George Bemis was our fellow-traveler.

(9) We had never seen him before. He wore in his belt an old original "Allen" revolver, such as irreverent people called a "pepper-box." Simply drawing the trigger back, cocked and fired the pistol. As the trigger came back, the hammer would begin to rise and the barrel to turn over, and presently down would drop the hammer, and away would speed the ball. To aim along the turning barrel and hit the thing aimed at was a feat which was probably never done with an "Allen" in the world. But George's was a reliable weapon, nevertheless, because, as one of the stage-drivers afterward said, "If she didn't get what she went after, she would fetch something else." And so she did. She went after a deuce of spades nailed against a tree, once, and fetched a mule standing about thirty yards to the left of it. Bemis did not want the mule; but the owner came out with a double-barreled shotgun and persuaded him to buy it, anyhow. It was a cheerful weapon—the "Allen." Sometimes all its six barrels would go off at once, and then there was no safe place in all the region round about, but behind it.

(10) We took two or three blankets for protection against frosty weather in the mountains. In the matter of luxuries we were modest—we took none along but some pipes and five pounds of smoking tobacco. We had two large canteens to carry water in, between stations on the Plains, and we also took with us a little shot-bag of silver coin for daily expenses in the way of breakfasts and dinners.

(11) By eight o'clock everything was ready, and we were on the other side of the river. We jumped into the stage, the driver cracked his whip, and we bowled away and left "the States" behind us. It was a superb summer morning, and all the landscape was brilliant with sunshine. There was a freshness and breeziness, too, and an exhilarating sense of emancipation from all sorts of cares and responsibilities, that almost made us feel that the years we had spent in the close, hot city, toiling and slaving, had been wasted and thrown away. We were spinning along through Kansas, and in the course of an hour and a half we were fairly abroad on the great Plains. Just here the land was rolling—a grand sweep of regular elevations and depressions as far as the eye could reach—like the stately heave and swell of the ocean's bosom after a storm. And everywhere were cornfields, accenting with squares of deeper green, this limitless expanse of grassy land. But presently

this sea upon dry ground was to lose its "rolling" character and stretch away for seven hundred miles as level as a floor!

(12) Our coach was a great swinging and swaying stage, of the most sumptuous description—an imposing cradle on wheels. It was drawn by six handsome horses, and by the side of the driver sat the "conductor," the legitimate captain of the craft; for it was his business to take charge and care of the mails, baggage, express matter, and passengers. We three were the only passengers, this trip. We sat on the back seat, inside. About all the rest of the coach was full of mail bags—for we had three days' delayed mails with us. Almost touching our knees, a perpendicular wall of mail matter rose up to the roof. There was a great pile of it strapped on top of the stage, and both the fore and hind boots were full. We had twenty-seven hundred pounds of it aboard, the driver said—"a little for Brigham, and Carson, and 'Frisco, but the heft of it for the Injuns, which is powerful troublesome 'thout they get plenty of truck to read."

(13) But as he just then got up a fearful convulsion of his countenance which was suggestive of a wink being swallowed by an earthquake, we guessed that his remark was intended to be facetious, and to mean that we would unload the most of our mail matter somewhere on the Plains and leave it to the Indians, or whosoever wanted it.

(14) We changed horses every ten miles, all day long, and fairly flew over the hard, level road. We jumped out and stretched our legs every time the coach stopped, and so the night found us still vivacious and unfatigued.

(15) After supper a woman got in, who lived about fifty miles further on, and we three had to take turns at sitting outside with the driver and conductor. Apparently she was not a talkative woman. She would sit there in the gathering twilight and fasten her steadfast eyes on a mosquito rooting into her arm, and slowly she would raise her other hand till she had got his range, and then she would launch a slap at him that would have jolted a cow; and after that she would sit and contemplate the corpse with tranquil satisfaction—for she never missed her mosquito; she was a dead shot at short range. She never removed a carcass, but left them there for bait. I sat by this grim Sphynx and watched her kill thirty or forty mosquitoes—watched her, and waited for her to say something, but she never did. So I finally opened the conversation myself. I said:

(16) "The mosquitoes are pretty bad, about here, madam."

(17) "You bet!"

(18) "What did I understand you to say, madam?"

(19) "You BET!"

(20) Then she cheered up, and faced around and said:

(21)"Danged if I didn't begin to think you fellers was deef and dumb. I did, b'gosh. Here I've sot, and sot, and sot, a-bust'n muskeeters and wonderin' what was ailin' ye. Fust I thot you was deef and dumb, then I thot you was sick or crazy, or suthin', and then by and by I begin to reckon you was a passel of sickly fools that couldn't think of nothing to say. Wher'd ye come from?"

(22) The Sphynx was a Sphynx no more! The fountains of her great deep were broken up, and she rained the nine parts of speech forty days and forty nights, metaphorically speaking, and buried us under a desolating deluge of trivial gossip that left not a crag or pinnacle of rejoinder projecting above the tossing waste of dislocated grammar and decomposed pronunciation!

(23) How we suffered, suffered, suffered! She went on, hour after hour, till I was sorry I ever opened the mosquito question and gave her a start. She never did stop again until she got to her journey's end toward daylight; and then she stirred us up as she was leaving the stage (for we were nodding, by that time), and said:

(24) "Now you git out at Cottonwood, you fellers, and lay over a couple o' days, and I'll be along some time to-night, and if I can do ye any good by edgin' in a word now and then, I'm right thar. Folks'll tell you't I've always ben kind o' offish and partic'lar for a gal that's raised in the woods, and I am, with the rag-tag and bob-tail, and a gal has to be, if she wants to be anything, but when people comes along which is my equals, I reckon I'm a pretty sociable heifer after all."

(25) We resolved not to "lay by at Cottonwood."

22. Read the following dictionary entry:

Retire v 1. To end a professional career 2. To withdraw from a situation in order to get more privacy 3. To go to bed 4. To give up an activity

Which definition best matches the way the word *retired* is used in paragraph 5?

a. Definition 1
b. Definition 2
c. Definition 3
d. Definition 4

23. What emotion or characteristic does the narrator show in paragraph 25?

a. Dry humor
b. Friendliness
c. Irritation
d. Amazement

24. In paragraph 13, the phrase "fearful convulsion of his countenance which was suggestive of a wink being swallowed by an earthquake" means that the driver is which of the below?

a. Scared
b. Laughing
c. Shaking
d. Swallowing

This question has two parts. Answer Part A, then answer Part B.

25. Part A: In paragraph 11, what does the word "bowled" mean?

a. To play the sport of bowling
b. To wear a bowler hat
c. To move quickly
d. To roll a ball

Part B: Which statement from the story gives you the best clue as to what the word "bowled" means?

a. the driver cracked his whip
b. we were on the other side of the river
c. left "the States" behind us
d. We jumped into the stage

26. Which sentence or phrase best helps the reader visualize the Plains?

a. We took two or three blankets for protection against frosty weather
b. The landscape was brilliant with sunshine
c. And in the course of an hour and a half we were fairly abroad on the great Plains.
d. But presently this sea upon dry ground was to lose its "rolling" character and stretch away for seven hundred miles as level as a floor.

27. In paragraph 8, what does "poor innocents" mean?

a. The narrator and his brother did not know the dangers they would face on the Plains.
b. The narrator and his brother didn't know they could purchase items in San Francisco.
c. The narrator and his brother didn't know that San Francisco is close to Carson City.
d. The narrator and his brother had run out of money and could not purchase supplies.

28. Which of these best conveys the narrator's sense of humor?

a. I was young and ignorant, and I envied my brother.
b. At the end of an hour or two I was ready for the journey.
c. I thought she wanted a pair of stilts
d. "The mosquitos are pretty bad, about here, madam."

29. Which of these is the best paraphrase of the dialogue in paragraph 21?

a. Well, if I wasn't thinking you guys couldn't hear or speak. I sat and sat and wondered what was the matter. First I thought you couldn't hear or speak, and then I thought you were crazy. And then I thought you were just sick.
b. Well, if I wasn't thinking you guys couldn't hear or speak. I sat and sat and wondered what was the matter. First I thought you couldn't hear or speak, and then I thought you were crazy or sick. And then I thought you just couldn't think of anything to say.
c. Well, if I wasn't thinking you guys were just deaf. I sat and sat and wondered what was the matter. First I thought you couldn't deaf, and then I thought you were crazy or sick. And then I thought you just couldn't think of anything to say.
d. Well, if I wasn't thinking you guys couldn't hear or speak. I saw the land pass by and wondered what was the matter. First I thought you couldn't hear or speak, and then I thought you were crazy or sick. And then I thought you just couldn't think of anything to say.

30. The narrator divides the passage into two chapters in order to:

a. end the first chapter on a cliffhanger
b. begin describing the journey in a new chapter
c. separate the two parts of the journey
d. make each section about the same length

31. Which of the choices below is the best summary of the selection?

a. The narrator travels to the Nevada Territory, first by rail and then by stagecoach. When he arrives, he meets a woman who lives in Cottonwood.
b. The narrator travels to the Nevada Territory in order to become the Secretary of Nevada Territory. He travels by steamship and stagecoach and describes his journey across the Plains.
c. The narrator travels to the Nevada Territory by the Pacific Railway in order to visit his brother. Along the way, he sees the Plains and meets interesting people.
d. The narrator travels to the Nevada Territory to work for his brother. He travels by steamship and then by stagecoach and describes his journey across the Plains.

Questions 32 – 41 pertain to Oregon, Washington and Alaska; Sights and Scenes for the Tourist:

The Project Gutenberg eBook: Oregon, Washington and Alaska; Sights and Scenes for the Tourist

By E. L. Lomax

(1) The native islanders called the mainland "Al-ay-ek-sa," which signifies "great country," and the word has been corrupted into "Alaska." This immense empire, it will be remembered, was sold by Russia to the United States October 18, 1867, for $7,500,000. The country was discovered by Vitus Behring in 1741. Alaska has an area of 578,000 square miles, and is nearly one-fifth as large as all the other States and Territories combined. It is larger than twelve States the size of New York.

(2) The best time to visit Alaska is from May to September. The latter month is usually lovely, and the sea beautifully smooth, but the days begin to grow short. The trip occupies about twenty-five days.

(3) As the rainfall in Alaska is usually very large, it naturally follows that an umbrella is a convenient companion. A gossamer for a lady and a mackintosh for a gentleman, and heavy shoes, and coarse, warm and comfortable clothing for both should be provided.

(4) There are no "Palace" hotels in Alaska. One will have no desire to remain over there a trip. The tourist goes necessarily when and where the steamer goes, will have an opportunity to see all there is of note or worth seeing in Southeastern Alaska. The steamer sometimes goes north as far as Chilcat, say up to about the 58th degree of north latitude. The pleasure is not so much in the stopping as in the going. One is constantly passing through new channels, past new islands, opening up new points of interest, until finally a surfeit of the grand and magnificent in nature is reached.

(5) A correspondent of a western journal signing himself "Emerald" has written a description of this Alaskan tour in September, 1888. It is so charmingly done, so fresh, so vivid, and so full of interesting detail, that it is given herewith entire:

(6) We have all thought we were fairly appreciative of the wealth and wonders of Uncle Sam's domain. At Niagara we have gloried in the belief that all the cataracts of other lands were tame; but we changed our mind when we stood on the brink of Great Shoshone Falls. In Yellowstone the proudest thought was that all the world's other similar wonders were commonplace; and at Yosemite's Inspiration Point the unspeakable thrill of awe and delight was richly heightened by the grand idea that there was no such majesty or glory beyond either sea. But after all this, we now know that it yet remains for the Alaskan trip to rightly round out one's appreciation and admiration of the size and grandeur of our native land.

(7) Some of our most delighted *voyageurs* are from Portland, Maine. When they had journeyed some 1,500 miles to Omaha they imagined themselves at least half way across our continent. Then, when they had finished that magnificent stretch of some 1,700 miles more from Omaha to Portland, Oregon, in the palace cars of the Union Pacific, they were quite sure of it. Of course, they confessed a sense of mingled disappointment and eager anticipation when they learned that they were yet less than half way. They learned what is a fact—that the extreme west coast of Alaska is as far west of Sitka as Portland, Maine, is east of Portland, Oregon, and the further fact that San Francisco lacks 4,000 miles of being as far west as Uncle Sam's "Land's End," at extreme Western Alaska. It is a great country; great enough to contain one river—the Yukon—about as large as the Mississippi, and a coast line about twice as long as all the balance of the United States. It is twelve times as large as the State of New York, with resources that astonish every visitor, and a climate not altogether bad, as some would have it. The greatest trouble is that during the eighteen years it has been linked to our chain of Territories it has been treated like a discarded offspring or outcast, cared for more by others than its lawful protector. But, like many a refugee, it is carving for itself a place which others will yet envy. But, to our trip.

(8) There are seven in our party, mainly from Chicago. After a week of delightful mountaineering at Idaho Springs, in Platte Cañon, and other Union Pacific resorts in Colorado, we indulged in that delicious plunge at Garfield Beach, Salt Lake, and, en route to Portland over the Union Pacific Ry., quaffed that all but nectar at Soda Springs, Idaho, and dropped off a day to take a peep, at Shoshone Falls, which, in all seriousness, have attractions of which even our great Niagara can not boast. We found that glorious dash down through the palisades of the Columbia, and the sail, through the entrancing waterways of Puget Sound, a fitting prelude to our recent Alaskan journey.

(9) The Alaskan voyage is like a continuous dream of pleasure, so placid and quiet are the waters of the landlocked sea and so exquisitely beautiful the environment. The route keeps along the east shore of Vancouver Island its entire length, through the Gulf of Georgia, Johnstone strait, and out into Queen Charlotte Sound, where is felt the first swell of old ocean, and our staunch steamship "Elder" was rocked in its cradle for about four hours. Oftentimes we seemed to be bound by mountains on every side, with no hope of escape; but the faithful deck officer on watch would give his orders in clear, full tones that brought the bow to some passage leading to the great beyond. In narrow straits the steamer had to wait for the tide; then would she weave in and

out, like a shuttle in a loom, among the buoys, leaving the black ones on the left and the red ones on the right, and ever and anon they would be in a straight line, with the wicked boulder-heads visible beneath the surface or lifting their savage points above, compelling almost a square corner to be turned in order to avoid them. At such times the passengers were all on deck, listening to the captain's commands, and watching the boat obey his bidding.

(10) From Victoria to Tongas Narrows the distance is 638 miles, and here was the first stop for the tourists...

(11) From Tongas Narrows to Fort Wrangel, thousands of islands fill the water, while the mainland is on the right and Prince of Wales Island on the extreme left.

Fort Wrangel

(12) Like all Alaska towns, it is situated at the base of lofty peaks along the water's edge at the head of moderately pretty harbors. It seems to be the generic home of storms, and the mountains, the rocks, the buildings, and trees, and all, show the weird workings of nature's wrath. In 1863 it was a thriving town where miners outfitted for the mines of the Stikeen river and Cassian mines of British Columbia; but that excitement has temporarily subsided, and the $150,000 government buildings are falling in decay. The streets are filled with debris, and everything betokens the ravages of time. The largest and most grotesque totem poles seen on the trip here towered a height of fifty feet. Those poles represent a history of the family and the ancestry as far as they can trace it. If they are of the Wolf tribe a huge wolf is carved at the top of the pole, and then on down with various signs to the base, the great events of the family and the intermarriages, not forgetting to give place to the good and bad gods who assisted them. The genealogy of a tribe is always traced back through the mother's side. The totem poles are sometimes very large, perhaps four feet at the base. When the carving is completed they are planted firmly in front of the hut, there to stay until they fall away. At the lower end, some four feet from the ground, there is an opening into the already hollowed pole, and in this are put the bones of the burned bodies of the family. It is only the wealthier families who support a totem pole, and no amount of money can induce an Indian to part with his family tree.

From Sights and Scenes for the Tourist by E.L. Lomax (Visual Representation)

The Private Hotel, Dining, Hunting and Sleeping Cars of the Pullman Company will accommodate from 12 to 18 persons, allowing a full bed to each, and are fitted with such modern conveniences as private, observation and smoking rooms, folding beds, reclining chairs, buffets and kitchens. They are "*just the thing*" for tourists, theatrical companies, sportsmen, and private parties. The Hunting Cars have special conveniences, being provided with dog-kennels, gun-racks, fishing-tackle, etc. These cars can be chartered at following rates per diem (the time being reckoned from date of departure until return of same, unless otherwise arranged with the Pullman Company):

Less than Ten Days

	per day		*per day*
Hotel Cars	$50.00	Private or Hunting Cars	$35.00
Buffet Cars	45.00	Private Cars with Buffet	30.00
Sleeping Cars	40.00	Dining Cars	30.00

Ten Days or over, $5.00 per day less than above. Hotel, Buffet, or Sleeping Cars can also be chartered for continuous trips without lay-over between points where extra cars are furnished (cars to be given up at destination), as follows:

Where berth rate is	$1.50,	car rate will be	$35.00.
Where berth rate is	2.00,	car rate will be	45.00.
Where berth rate is	2.50,	car rate will be	55.00.

For each additional berth rate of 50 cents, car rate will be increased $10.00.

Above rates include service of polite and skillful attendants. The commissariat will also be furnished if desired. Such chartered cars must contain not less than 15 persons holding full first-class tickets, and another full fare ticket will be required for each additional passenger over 15. If chartered "per diem" cars are given up *en route*, chartering party must arrange for return to original starting point free, or pay amount of freight necessary for return thereto. Diagrams showing interior of these cars can be had of any agent of the Company.

32. What can the reader infer is a difference between Portland, Maine, and Portland, Oregon?

a. The two Portlands are on opposite sides of the United States.
b. The two Portlands are on the same coast of the United States.
c. The two Portlands are in different states.
d. Passengers can take the train from Portland, Oregon, but not from Portland, Maine.

33. In paragraph 9, what does the word "landlocked" mean?

a. A sea that is on land
b. The Pacific Ocean
c. The Atlantic Ocean
d. A sea surrounded entirely by land

34. Which of these best summarizes paragraphs 8-12?

a. A group of travelers set off for Alaska, making several stops along the way. The group stopped at Fort Wrangel, which is a thriving mining town. The town has many totem poles, which represent the family tree for the Indians who live near Fort Wrangel.
b. A group of travelers set off for Alaska, making several stops along the way. The group stopped at Fort Wrangel, which was a thriving mining town but is now in decline. The town has many totem poles, which represent the family tree for the Indians who live near Fort Wrangel.
c. A group of travelers set off for Alaska, making several stops along the way, including in Chicago. The group stopped at Fort Wrangel, which was a thriving mining town but is now in decline. The town has many totem poles, which represent the family tree for the Indians who live near Fort Wrangel.
d. A group of travelers set off for Alaska, making several stops along the 638-mile route. The group stopped at Fort Wrangel, which is a thriving mining town. The town has many totem poles, which represent the family tree for the Indians who live near Fort Wrangel.

35. What is the definition of "voyageur" in paragraph 7?

a. Voyage
b. Trip
c. Travel
d. Traveler

This question has two parts. Answer Part A, then answer Part B.

36. Part A: What is the main purpose of paragraph 7?

a. To convey the awe and delight the group felt at seeing the sights of Alaska
b. To describe the people in the group
c. To show the great distance and size of Alaska
d. To describe how Alaska has been treated like a discarded offspring

Part B: Which sentence from paragraph 7 supports your answer in Part A?

a. It is a great country; great enough to contain one river—the Yukon—about as large as the Mississippi, and a coast line about twice as long as all the balance of the United States.
b. Some of our most delighted *voyageurs* are from Portland, Maine.
c. But, like many a refugee, it is carving for itself a place which others will yet envy.
d. Of course, they confessed a sense of mingled disappointment and eager anticipation when they learned that they were yet less than half way.

37. What is the most logical reason why there are no "Palace" hotels in Alaska?

a. There is no royalty living in Alaska.
b. The sights in Alaska are mostly based around nature.
c. It rains too much.
d. The days are too short.

38. Which phrase best demonstrates the author's opinion about Alaska?

a. The unspeakable thrill of awe and delight was richly heightened by the grand idea that there was no such majesty or glory beyond either sea.
b. They had finished that magnificent stretch
c. It is a great country.
d. Like a continuous dream of pleasure

39. What do the totem poles at Fort Wrangel represent?

a. The prosperity of Fort Wrangel
b. The decline of Fort Wrangel
c. The lineage of Native American families who live around Fort Wrangel
d. The family and ancestry of Fort Wrangel's recent settlers

40. Which sentence or phrase best conveys the huge size of Alaska?

a. They had journeyed some 1,500 miles
b. They had finished that magnificent stretch of some 1,700 miles
c. 4,000 miles of being as far west as Uncle Sam's "Land's End"
d. Coast line about twice as long as all the balance of the United States

41. The reader can infer that:

a. the passage describes the end of a 25-day voyage
b. the passage describes the beginning of a visit to Alaska
c. the voyagers have traveled to Alaska many times
d. the narrator has never been to Alaska

Use Roughing It and Oregon, Washington and Alaska; Sights and Scenes for the Tourist to answer questions 42-44:

42. What topic do both selections have in common?

a. Companionship
b. History
c. Travel
d. Natural wonders

43. What characteristic does the narrators from both passages share?

a. Excitement
b. Irritation
c. Boredom
d. Prior experience

This question has two parts. Answer Part A, then answer Part B.

44. Part A: Both selections have a large amount of which of the following?

a. Dialogue
b. Internal thought
c. Humor
d. Description

Part B: Give an example from each selection that supports your answer in Part A.

____

____

____

____

Use the visual representation to answer questions 45-47:

45. If someone wants to charter a hotel car for fifteen days, the cost per day will be which of the following?

a. $40
b. $45
c. $50
d. $675

46. The most likely purpose of this passage is to

a. tell a passenger how much he or she owes for a trip
b. show the cost of a first-class ticket
c. present the different rates passengers might pay while riding the railroad
d. give a diagram showing the interior of the cars

47. Which of these would be least likely to charter a sleeping car?

a. A group taking a continuous trip
b. A theater troupe
c. A group of tourists
d. A private individual

Short answer question

In what way does the story in *Roughing It* illustrate why the author chose this title? Explain your answer and support it with evidence from the selection.

Questions 48 -56 pertain to the following passages:

Alice's Adventures in Wonderland

By Lewis Carroll

(1) Alice was beginning to get very tired of sitting by her sister on the bank, and of having nothing to do: once or twice she had peeped into the book her sister was reading, but it had no pictures or conversations in it, 'and what is the use of a book,' thought Alice 'without pictures or conversation?'

(2) So she was considering in her own mind (as well as she could, for the hot day made her feel very sleepy and stupid), whether the pleasure of making a daisy-chain would be worth the trouble of getting up and picking the daisies, when suddenly a White Rabbit with pink eyes ran close by her.

(3) There was nothing so VERY remarkable in that; nor did Alice think it so VERY much out of the way to hear the Rabbit say to itself, 'Oh dear! Oh dear! I shall be late!' (when she thought it over afterwards, it occurred to her that she ought to have wondered at this, but at the time it all seemed quite natural); but when the Rabbit actually TOOK A WATCH OUT OF ITS WAISTCOAT-POCKET, and looked at it, and then hurried on, Alice started to her feet, for it flashed across her mind that she had never before seen a rabbit with either a waistcoat-pocket, or a watch to take out of it, and burning with curiosity, she ran across the field after it, and fortunately was just in time to see it pop down a large rabbit-hole under the hedge.

(4) In another moment down went Alice after it, never once considering how in the world she was to get out again.

(5) The rabbit-hole went straight on like a tunnel for some way, and then dipped suddenly down, so suddenly that Alice had not a moment to think about stopping herself before she found herself falling down a very deep well.
(6) Either the well was very deep, or she fell very slowly, for she had plenty of time as she went down to look about her and to wonder what was going to happen next. First, she tried to look down and make out what she was coming to, but it was too dark to see anything; then she looked at the sides of the well, and noticed that they were filled with cupboards and book-shelves; here and there she saw maps and pictures hung upon pegs. She took down a jar from one of the shelves as she passed; it was labelled 'ORANGE MARMALADE', but to her great disappointment it was empty: she did not like to drop the jar for fear of killing somebody, so managed to put it into one of the cupboards as she fell past it.
(7) 'Well!' thought Alice to herself, 'after such a fall as this, I shall think nothing of tumbling down stairs! How brave they'll all think me at home! Why, I wouldn't say anything about it, even if I fell off the top of the house!' (Which was very likely true.)
(8) Down, down, down. Would the fall NEVER come to an end! 'I wonder how many miles I've fallen by this time?' she said aloud. 'I must be getting somewhere near the centre of the earth. Let me see: that would be four thousand miles down, I think—' (for, you see, Alice had learnt several things of this sort in her lessons in the schoolroom, and though this was not a VERY good opportunity for showing off her knowledge, as there was no one to listen to her, still it was good practice to say it over) '—yes, that's about the right distance—but then I wonder what Latitude or Longitude I've got to?' (Alice had no idea what Latitude was, or Longitude either, but thought they were nice grand words to say.)
(9) Presently she began again. 'I wonder if I shall fall right THROUGH the earth! How funny it'll seem to come out among the people that walk with their heads downward! The Antipathies, I think—' (she was rather glad there WAS no one listening, this time, as it didn't sound at all the right word) '—but I shall have to ask them what the name of the country is, you know. Please, Ma'am, is this New Zealand or Australia?' (and she tried to curtsey as she spoke—fancy CURTSEYING as you're falling through the air! Do you think you could manage it?) 'And what an ignorant little girl she'll think me for asking! No, it'll never do to ask: perhaps I shall see it written up somewhere.'
(10) Down, down, down. There was nothing else to do, so Alice soon began talking again. 'Dinah'll miss me very much to-night, I should think!' (Dinah was the cat.) 'I hope they'll remember her saucer of milk at tea-time. Dinah my dear! I wish you were down here with me! There are no mice in the air, I'm afraid, but you might catch a bat, and that's very like a mouse, you know. But do cats eat bats, I wonder?' And here Alice began to get rather sleepy, and went on saying to herself, in a dreamy sort of way, 'Do cats eat bats? Do cats eat bats?' and sometimes, 'Do bats eat cats?' for, you see, as she couldn't answer either question, it didn't much matter which way she put it. She felt that she was dozing off, and had just begun to dream that she was walking hand in hand with Dinah, and saying to her very earnestly, 'Now, Dinah, tell me the truth: did you ever eat a bat?' when suddenly, thump! thump! down she came upon a heap of sticks and dry leaves, and the fall was over.
(11) Alice was not a bit hurt, and she jumped up on to her feet in a moment: she looked up, but it was all dark overhead; before her was another long passage, and the White Rabbit was still in sight, hurrying down it. There was not a moment to be lost: away went Alice like the wind, and was just in time to hear it say, as it turned a corner, 'Oh my ears and whiskers, how late it's getting!' She was close behind it

when she turned the corner, but the Rabbit was no longer to be seen: she found herself in a long, low hall, which was lit up by a row of lamps hanging from the roof.
(12) There were doors all round the hall, but they were all locked; and when Alice had been all the way down one side and up the other, trying every door, she walked sadly down the middle, wondering how she was ever to get out again.
(13) Suddenly she came upon a little three-legged table, all made of solid glass; there was nothing on it except a tiny golden key, and Alice's first thought was that it might belong to one of the doors of the hall; but, alas! either the locks were too large, or the key was too small, but at any rate it would not open any of them. However, on the second time round, she came upon a low curtain she had not noticed before, and behind it was a little door about fifteen inches high: she tried the little golden key in the lock, and to her great delight it fitted!
(14) Alice opened the door and found that it led into a small passage, not much larger than a rat-hole: she knelt down and looked along the passage into the loveliest garden you ever saw. How she longed to get out of that dark hall, and wander about among those beds of bright flowers and those cool fountains, but she could not even get her head through the doorway; 'and even if my head would go through,' thought poor Alice, 'it would be of very little use without my shoulders. Oh, how I wish I could shut up like a telescope! I think I could, if I only know how to begin.' For, you see, so many out-of-the-way things had happened lately, that Alice had begun to think that very few things indeed were really impossible.
(15) There seemed to be no use in waiting by the little door, so she went back to the table, half hoping she might find another key on it, or at any rate a book of rules for shutting people up like telescopes: this time she found a little bottle on it, ('which certainly was not here before,' said Alice,) and round the neck of the bottle was a paper label, with the words 'DRINK ME' beautifully printed on it in large letters.
(16) It was all very well to say 'Drink me,' but the wise little Alice was not going to do THAT in a hurry. 'No, I'll look first,' she said, 'and see whether it's marked "poison" or not'; for she had read several nice little histories about children who had got burnt, and eaten up by wild beasts and other unpleasant things, all because they WOULD not remember the simple rules their friends had taught them: such as, that a red-hot poker will burn you if you hold it too long; and that if you cut your finger VERY deeply with a knife, it usually bleeds; and she had never forgotten that, if you drink much from a bottle marked 'poison,' it is almost certain to disagree with you, sooner or later.
(17) However, this bottle was NOT marked 'poison,' so Alice ventured to taste it, and finding it very nice, (it had, in fact, a sort of mixed flavour of cherry-tart, custard, pine-apple, roast turkey, toffee, and hot buttered toast,) she very soon finished it off.
(18) 'What a curious feeling!' said Alice; 'I must be shutting up like a telescope.'
(19) And so it was indeed: she was now only ten inches high, and her face brightened up at the thought that she was now the right size for going through the little door into that lovely garden. First, however, she waited for a few minutes to see if she was going to shrink any further: she felt a little nervous about this; 'for it might end, you know,' said Alice to herself, 'in my going out altogether, like a candle. I wonder what I should be like then?' And she tried to fancy what the flame of a candle is like after the candle is blown out, for she could not remember ever having seen such a thing.

48. Read the following dictionary entry:

Burning [bur-ning] adjective (1) intense or urgent (2) very hot (3) on fire, with visible flames (4) a feeling caused by some kind of fire or heat

Which definition best matches the meaning of "burning" as it is used in paragraph 3?

a. Definition 1
b. Definition 2
c. Definition 3
d. Definition 4

49. How does the setting at the beginning of the story contribute to Alice's decision to follow the White Rabbit?

a. It makes her feel sleepy
b. It makes her feel restless
c. It makes her feel curious
d. It makes her feel like reading

50. Why might Alice use the words *latitude* and *longitude* in paragraph 8?

a. She wants to find her exact location on the map.
b. She wants to show off her knowledge of big words.
c. She wants to see if her words echo down the hole.
d. She wants to say big words even if she doesn't know exactly what they mean.

51. Why has the author capitalized the words *through*, *was*, and *curtseying* in paragraph 9?

a. To mark them as words that need to be proofread
b. To emphasize their meaning
c. To show that Alice is upset by falling
d. To indicate that Alice is talking to someone

52. Alice's decision to drink the liquid in the bottle in paragraphs 15-17 can be described as...

a. Thoughtful
b. Angry
c. Wild
d. Unreasonable

53. Why does Alice feel nervous in paragraph 19?

a. She thinks the liquid might be poison
b. She is afraid that the liquid isn't working
c. She is worried that she will keep shrinking
d. She is nervous that she will turn into a flame

This question has two parts. Answer Part A, then answer Part B.

54. From the description in paragraphs 6-10, the reader can tell that...

a. Alice is in great danger
b. Alice is very nervous
c. The story will be realistic
d. The story will be fantastical

Part B: Which sentence from paragraphs 6-10 best supports your answer in Part A?

a. How brave they'll all think me at home!
b. Presently she began again.
c. 'And what an ignorant little girl she'll think me for asking!
d. 'I wonder if I shall fall right THROUGH the earth!

55. What is Alice's problem in paragraph 14?

a. She can't fit the key into any of the doors
b. She can't fit through the door that the key opens
c. She is shrinking
d. She is in a strange, unknown setting

56. What is the author indicating is most unusual about the rabbit described in paragraphs 2 and 3?

a. It has pink eyes
b. It is speaking
c. It has a watch
d. It jumps down a rabbit hole

Questions 57 – 60 pertain to the following letter:

Letters from an Oklahoman Abroad

By Carrie LeFlore Perry

Montreal

Mother Mine:

(1) Out of the United States! We passed across the lake from Lewiston to Toronto and finding a couple of hours at our disposal, we proceeded to "do" the town. I cannot say it is especially interesting; it is clean and hustling, but too much like an American city to please me. You see, I am looking for the old, the beautiful and the picturesque, not the new and practical. The night was so cool I slept like a child and awoke at five-thirty ready to enjoy the Thousand Islands. I think a picture of an openmouthed rustic and a whole row of exclamation points would give you a better idea of my state this morning than words. Island after island, bearing homes of splendor, then dear little wooded spots with an unpretentious cottage peeping from the trees; again, a monster club house and magnificent grounds, just one continuous picture of homes and places of pleasure. Many of the houses crowning the islands were such monster affairs the lawns were lost in the river! Do they have babies in those homes? If so, how do they keep them out of the water? Ed chuckled with pleasure over the mental picture of you, on a little pocket-handkerchief lawn, with those irrepressible boys, in a wild endeavor to keep them out of the St. Lawrence!

(2) The early morning light added to the magic beauty of the scene, yet I shall be disappointed if the Rhine is not more entrancing.

(3) The castles are too new, the homes do not show the caress of time; it is like our entire country, great and beautiful, but so new, so palpably new. We were from six to

ten-thirty passing through this wonderful bit of the St. Lawrence, and like unto children, we were quite sure the island of the moment was the most fair.

(4) We were told that there were 1,642 in all, and I do not doubt the statement after this morning. Leaving Prescott where we changed to a smaller boat, we were soon passing the numerous rapids. They increased in wonder until the Lachine Rapids were entered, and there we were truly amazed! A lady friend had informed me that I would be greatly disappointed with the rapids, as they were very peaceful, like unto soap bubbles! My comment is this: I would not wish that brand of soap turned loose in my vicinity if I were boating. Do you recall the legend of the Indian, who, for telling a lie, was doomed by the Great Spirit to ever wander by streams with his canoe upon his back in a fruitless search for a place to launch it? I wonder if he ever tried the Lachine Rapids? If he did I'll venture the Great Spirit had to hurry to save man and canoe. When we reached Cornwall, we found the bridge had fallen, blocking the canal, and learned our boat would be the last to Montreal for several days. You see the vessels go down the river but up the canal, because of the rapids. I am so thankful we did not miss our river trip.

(5) We are staying at a quaint old hotel, in the French part of the city, very near the cathedral where Ed was christened. You need a guide in the hotel; it is a succession of up you go and down you come! There is an air of age and an odor too, about the rooms and corridors. We were told the present King stayed here, when he visited Canada as Prince of Wales, and I feel sure there has been little change since then! We have a monster apartment lined with mirrors and such massive furniture I feel oppressed. I tried to find the office before commencing this letter, and landed in an unknown hall. Seeing a chambermaid I inquired the way to the elevator, and was told something like this: Up two stairs, around a corner, down three steps, a long corridor, up three, then up two, across a hall, and enter the elevator and I would soon find myself opposite the office! I appreciated her directions but begged her to escort me to room 45 as I would defer the excursion until my husband returned.

(6) I wish I could find my way to the hall of the lion; it is rather exciting to press a button, see the monster tongue loll out, and then a stream of ice water. Would not the boys drink to repletion?

June 24

(7) Mother, Ed came in just as I was finishing the above paragraph, and with his assistance I found the lion and also enjoyed a street car ride. Today we have been "sight-seeing." Right here I wish to say that Ed would be a capital guide, he will even sacrifice truth to interest if he is not sure of his data. You would never suspect it, but I have a lurking suspicion that I have been told many dream tales, although what of it? May not a man romance of his home city? The very first thing we did was to make our way across the historic Place D'Armes Square into the old cathedral. It is a place of shadows, where prayer comes easily to the heart; beneath the giant crucifix of our Lord thereon, the soul is melted with tenderness.

(8) I did so wish to examine the records and see his name there, as a tiny infant, but we were too early, and later in the day we would be elsewhere. We had decided to have breakfast in the Café A--, where Ed assured me the delicacies offered were beyond compare, and the room a little palace. Ah, the eyes of childhood! When we

entered the small place, Ed with a twinkle said: "My dear, this place has grown smaller; I assure you it used to be the size of the cathedral!" Dear old café, perhaps it had seen better days; I know I have never seen a poorer breakfast. I drank to the King, in a cup of awful liquid called English Breakfast tea. Heaven pity the subjects of King Edward if they drink that decoction frequently! After a most unsatisfactory repast Ed said: "Now we will buy the very finest peppermints in the world; the kind I used to eat." Alas for the dreams of childhood, the candy was the "last straw." When we reached the street it was my turn and I said, "Let us buy presidents at a baker shop, you know dear, the kind you used to buy in old Montreal." You see I was determined to finish the "dream" right then and there. Cruel of me, I hear you say? Do believe me, that pastry was delicious, the very best ever; I shall urge all my friends to visit Montreal and eat "Presidents." We walked on old Bleury Street to the Jesuit College where his young ideas were encourage to burst into bloom, and there I met an old priest who knew Ed as a boy, and had the pleasure (?) of teaching him. He assured me that Ed's ideas were always ready to bloom and ofttimes the flowers were startling.

(9) No one feared he would die early because of his angelic goodness, but they often expected him to enter the pearly gates in a violent manner. He was permitted to lead me through his former class room, recreation room, and out-door play grounds; it was quite interesting to see the places and hear his animated tales of old school days.

(10) From the College to Mount Royal on the cars it is but a little time, and there we were high above the city, enjoying the wondrous panorama. Ed pointed out all the historic houses and thus I have learned my Montreal fairly well, even if here but a day. This is a city of churches and charitable institutions, if we had more time we would surely visit many of them; I am not fully content with a "bird's eye view." When we returned to the hotel, while I rested Ed went out to see a college chum who is now a dignified attorney; he must have had a jolly time as he was quite late returning to the hotel for me, and our little excursion to the Convent of the Ladies of the Sacred Heart was begun as the afternoon was almost ended.

(11) The trolley ride was so cool and through such fine country I was rather sorry when the convent cross appeared. Madame K., my old teacher, gave us welcome and showed us the many beauties of the place. It was such a comfort to talk with dear Madam, I felt that she was truly interested in all that concerned me. After a pleasant hour, we turned our faces towards Montreal; the lamps were glowing when we reached the city and thus our pleasure was enhanced, it lies so quaint and queer under the gleaming lights. After a dinner--not at the Café A.--we strolled along the streets of the French town and Ed aired his mother-tongue with the many children scampering here and there in the joys of hide and seek. Thus ends our day in Montreal; we are true birds of passage, in twenty minutes we leave for Quebec, and until then you will have peace.

Lovingly,

C.

57. In paragraph 8, the word "repast" refers to...

a. English Breakfast tea
b. Breakfast
c. Peppermints
d. King Edward

This question has two parts. Answer Part A, then answer Part B.

58. Part A: Paragraphs 1-3 are mainly about the narrator...

a. Sightseeing across the United States
b. Exploring the castles along the Rhine river
c. Going down the St. Lawrence river to see both mansions and cottages
d. Watching children play in the river

Part B: Which sentence from the letter best supports your answer from Part A?

a. We passed across the lake from Lewiston to Toronto and finding a couple of hours at our disposal, we proceeded to "do" the town.
b. Island after island, bearing homes of splendor, then dear little wooded spots with an unpretentious cottage peeping from the trees; again, a monster club house and magnificent grounds, just one continuous picture of homes and places of pleasure.
c. Out of the United States!
d. If so, how do they keep them out of the water?

59. Why does the narrator find the "Thousand Islands" to be disappointing?

a. She thinks that the homes don't look old enough
b. She is displeased that the cottages and castles are so old
c. She is angry that the name of the islands is the Thousand Islands when there are really 1,642 islands
d. There were too many children around

60. How did the narrator learn about Montreal?

a. By touring the Thousand Islands
b. By eating at Café A
c. By viewing the city from Mount Royal
d. By chatting with Madame K.

Answers and Explanations

1. B: The passage discusses Helen Keller's life beginning with her birth and continuing on into her adulthood.

2. A: Although all of the answer choices are true, only choice A focuses on both Helen's journey to overcome her disabilities and Anne Sullivan's involvement.

3. D: The passage does mention that Helen graduated from Radcliffe College (choice A), and the passage does tell about Anne's role as Helen's teacher (choice B), but the passage as a whole does not focus on Helen's time at college or Anne's life outside of her role as teacher. The passage does not mention services available for the deaf and blind (choice C). The passage does tell about Helen Keller's life.

4. C: The second paragraph explains why Anne Sullivan was crucial to Helen's life, and the third paragraph elaborates on how Anne helped Helen succeed.

5. C: The author's use of the phrase "Helen learned at an incredible rate" and the word "remarkable" to describe Helen's life are two examples of the author's admiration.

6. Part A: B: The passage states: "Helen herself was easily frustrated and lonely in her dark, silent world." Being unable to see or hear left Helen with no alternatives for communication beyond temper tantrums. It was not until Anne Sullivan became Helen's teacher that Helen learned to communicate her thoughts in a positive way.

Part B: C: In the story it says that she would "have unpredictable outbursts of temper". It does not mention anything about any if the other answer choices.

7. D: Although all of the answer choices represent major events in Helen's life, the passage specifies that the advent of Anne Sullivan was the turning point in Helen's life when she began to learn to communicate with other people. "All of that began to change in March 1887 when Anne Sullivan came to live with the Kellers and be Helen's teacher. Anne taught Helen to communicate by forming letters with her fingers held in another person's hand."

8. A: The passage does not indicate that Helen's parents were jealous of Anne (choice B), glad to give Anne responsibility for Helen (choice C), or had any preference in their daughter's choice of a college (choice D). The passage does say that Helen's parents loved her and that they brought Anne to their home to be Helen's teacher. This implies that they were frustrated by their own inability to help Helen and were looking for someone who could.

9. A: "This connection engendered an insatiable curiosity within Helen." The context of this sentence indicates that the connection Helen made between words and the objects they represent caused an insatiable curiosity to exist within Helen.

10. C: "This connection engendered an insatiable curiosity within Helen. After that day, Helen learned at an incredible rate with Teacher by her side." The context of these sentences indicates that Helen's curiosity compelled her to keep learning because her curiosity would never be satisfied.

11. B: The passage does not say that studying a foreign language will help students find jobs after high school (choice A) or gain an understanding of other cultures (choice C). The passage does say that studying a foreign language is important for college acceptance (choice D), but this point alone is not the main idea of the passage.

12. C: The passage does not claim that studying a foreign language is essential to high school graduation (choice A). Choices B and D represent claims made in the passage, but do not include all of the claims made.

13. D: Although students may find knowledge of a foreign language helpful in obtaining a job, it is an obvious exaggeration to claim that students who did not study a foreign language would be unemployable.

14. D: Choices A and C represent options that would provide information regarding the opinions of students and parents, but not actual evidence regarding the influence of studying a foreign language on future success. Choice B specifies a second language taught at home, whereas the passage focuses specifically on a foreign language taught in high school.

15. B: Choices A, C, and D do not offer a complete summary of the claims made in this passage.

16. C: The selection does not portray the themes offered in choices A, B, and D.

17. A: Choice B is incorrect because Mother did not forbid any presents. Choices C and D give some of the problems presented in the selection, but do not offer a complete summary.

18. D: The passage states: "'We haven't got Father, and shall not have him for a long time.' She didn't say 'perhaps never,' but each silently added it, thinking of Father far away, where the fighting was." The other choices may be true of Father, but they are not specified in this selection.

19. C: Although choices A and B may be true, they are not specified in this selection. Jo believes choice D to be true, but whether or not she is right is not stated: "'Mother didn't say anything about our money, and she won't wish us to give up everything. Let's each buy what we want, and have a little fun; I'm sure we work hard enough to earn it,' cried Jo."

20. D: The other sisters all specify what they want to buy. Choice A: "'I shall get a nice box of Faber's drawing pencils; I really need them,' said Amy decidedly." Choice B: "'I planned to spend mine in new music,' said Beth." Choice C: "'I do want to buy Undine and Sintran for myself. I've wanted it so long,' said Jo."

21. D: The presence of a hearth brush and kettle-holder indicate a fireplace, and the fact that the fireplace "hears" Beth's sigh when no one else does indicates that Beth is closest to it.

22. D: is the correct answer because the context of the sentence shows that the travelers tried to get past the reefs and then gave up and found another route. Choice A is a common definition of the word *retire*, but this paragraph is not talking about someone who is retiring from a job. Instead, the narrator is describing how he and the other travelers withdrew from a task. Choice B is incorrect because the travelers didn't withdraw in order to get more privacy. Instead, they gave up because they couldn't get around the reefs. Choice C is incorrect because the travelers are not attempting to go to bed; instead, they are trying to travel down the river.

23. A: The narrator's dry humor is shown because he politely states he's not going to stop in Cottonwood, but he's really poking fun at the talkative woman. The statement shows that the travelers are not going to stop at Cottonwood because they don't want to spend any more time with the woman. Choice B is incorrect because the narrator shows the opposite of friendliness; he does not want to spend any more time with the woman and decides not to go to Cottonwood. Choice C is incorrect because the author is no longer irritated by the woman. He and his brother suffered through her conversation, but he's not angry; he simply does not want to spend additional time with her. Although the narrator is amazed by the woman's talkativeness in paragraph 22, he is no longer amazed by paragraph 25, making choice D incorrect. Instead, he jokes about his decision not to stop in Cottonwood.

24. B: because the driver is clearly making a joke and laughing. The narrator shows this by saying that the driver is being facetious. The narrator uses such a long phrase to describe the laugh because he's using humorous wording to describe the driver's expression. Although the phrase uses the word *fearful*, choice A is incorrect because the narrator uses *fearful* to imply that the expression looked a little scary. He does not mean that the driver is scared. Choice C is incorrect because the narrator uses *earthquake* to describe the crags of the driver's face and not the shaking of the earth that occurs during an earthquake. Choice D is incorrect because the driver is not swallowing; instead, his face is so creased that it looks like his wink is drowned out by the "earthquake".

25. Part A: C: because the sentence shows that the stage is moving quickly across the land. Choices A and C are incorrect because the word *bowl* in this passage does not refer to the sport of bowling. Instead, it refers to a way of moving. Choice B is incorrect because the author does not mention a hat or any other items of clothing.

Part B: C: In the story, they bowled away and "left "the States" behind us". This lets the reader know that they are leaving the states and they can infer that they are doing it rather quickly.

26. D: because the sentence shows that the Plains had a rolling or hilly character and then became very flat, or as level as a floor. Choice A is incorrect because the frosty weather discussed in paragraph 10 refers to the mountains rather than the Plains. Choice B is incorrect because the sentence simply talks about the sunny weather but does not help the reader understand or visualize what the Plains look like. Choice C is incorrect because the sentence describes the group's location but not the physical characteristics of the Plains.

27. B: because the narrator's brother brought items like an unabridged dictionary because he didn't know he could easily order them from San Francisco. The narrator uses the phrase *poor innocents* jokingly, but he means to say that he and his brother were ignorant of the opportunities in Carson City. Choice A is incorrect because the narrator is talking about purchasing items like a dictionary in this sentence rather than the dangers of travel. Choice C is incorrect because it only describes part of the narrator's meaning. The narrator and his brother may not have known that San Francisco was close to Carson City, but they also didn't know they could buy items from San Francisco. Choice D is incorrect because the word *poor* does not mean that the narrator and his brother don't have money. Instead, it means to be unfortunate or unlucky because they didn't know they could simply purchase the items in San Francisco.

28. C: because the phrase from paragraph 6 shows the narrator's dry sense of humor. Instead of simply stating that the boat needed a better way to get through the river, he makes a joke about stilts. Choice A is incorrect because the sentence shows the narrator's emotions (that he envies his brother) but is not humorous. Choice B is incorrect because the sentence simply states how long it took the author to get ready for the trip. Choice D is incorrect because the narrator is making an observation about the mosquitoes and is not making a joke.

29. B: While all of the answer choices have correct aspects, choice B is the only answer choice that is completely correct. Choice A is incorrect because the woman's final conclusion is not that the travelers were sick; she thought they were fools who couldn't think of anything to say. Choice C is incorrect because she didn't just think they were deaf. She also thought they were "dumb", which means she thought they couldn't speak. Choice D is incorrect because the woman doesn't say that she saw the land pass by. Instead, she says she "sot", which means to sit.

30. C: is the correct answer because the second chapter begins by describing the next stage of the journey to Carson City. Choice A is incorrect because Chapter 1 does not end with a cliffhanger, or a moment of anticipation. Choice B is incorrect because Chapter 1 shows the beginning of the journey. Choice D is incorrect because chapter 2 is about twice as long as Chapter 1.

31. D: While all of the answer choices have some parts that are correct, choice D is the only choice that summarizes the passage completely accurately. Choice A is incorrect because the narrator has not yet arrived in Nevada Territory when he meets the woman; he's still traveling. Choice B is incorrect because the narrator's brother is becoming the Secretary of Nevada Territory; the narrator is going to become his brother's private secretary. Choice C is incorrect because the narrator takes a stagecoach rather than the train because the Pacific Railway had not been built at the time of the journey.

32. A: because the passage says in paragraph 7 that Portland, Maine, is far to the east while Portland, Oregon, is located far to the west. Choice B is incorrect because paragraph 7 indicates that the two Portlands are very far apart. While it's true that the two Portlands are in different states, choice C is incorrect because the passage states this fact outright; the reader does not need to infer this difference. Choice D is incorrect because paragraph 7 says that the travelers did take the train from Maine.

33. D: because to be landlocked means to be surrounded on all sides by land. Choices B and C are incorrect because the passage doesn't say that the boat went through the Pacific or Atlantic Oceans. Choice A is incorrect because it is an illogical choice; as a body of water, a sea cannot be on land.

34. B: is the correct answer because paragraphs 8 and 9 talk about how the travelers set off for the trip to Alaska. Paragraph 12 talks about the group's arrival at Fort Wrangel and describes how it used to be a mining town and is now in decline. Paragraph 12 also says that the totem poles represent the family tree of different Indian families. The other choices are all partially correct but have some incorrect details. Choice A is incorrect because Fort Wrangel is no longer a thriving mining town. Choice C is incorrect because the group did not stop in Chicago; instead, many of the travelers are from Chicago. Choice D has two incorrect statements. First, the route to Alaska is much longer than 638 miles; only the portion from Victoria to Tongas Narrows is 638 miles. Second, Fort Wrangel is no longer a thriving town; it is in decline.

35. D: traveler, as shown by the context of the first sentence in paragraph 7. The sentence talks about how the travelers, or voyageurs, are from Portland, Maine, and how they journeyed across the country. Although the word *voyageur* contains the word *voyage,* the definitions of the word are slightly different. The word *voyage* means a trip while *voyageur* means the person who makes the trip. Therefore, choices A and B are both incorrect. Choice C is incorrect because the word *travel* can either be a verb that means to journey somewhere or a noun that refers to a trip.

36. Part A: C: Paragraph 7 mostly gives specific details showing how far away Alaska is from the mainland (such as in the phrase that says *they were yet less than half way*) and showing Alaska's immense size (such as in the phrase *coast line about twice as long as all the balance of the United States*). Choice A is incorrect because the group is not yet in Alaska in this paragraph. Instead, they are journeying towards the territory and learning how big it is. Although the paragraph does give some details about people in the group, such as the hometown of some of the travelers, the majority of the paragraph focuses on the location and size of Alaska. Choice D is incorrect because just the last sentence talks about how Alaska has been treated like a discarded offspring. The main part of the paragraph talks about the size and distance of the territory.

Part B: A: This sentence gives an example of how big Alaska is.

37. B: Although the author does not explicitly state that Alaska is an undeveloped territory with large tracts of nature, the author does give many details about the natural wonders of the territory. Therefore, the most logical reason to journey to Alaska is to see the natural sights and not stay at a "Palace" hotel or resort like location. Choice A is incorrect because "Palace" hotel is referring to a grand hotel, not a palace where royals live. Choice C is incorrect because the detail in paragraph 3 that it rains in Alaska is not related to the detail about the lack of "Palace" hotels. The discussion of the hotels comes in the next paragraph and talks about how travelers will constantly journey by steamer to see the different natural sights of the territory. Choice D is incorrect because the length of the days is not related to whether or not there is a hotel. Instead, the nature of the sights determines the types of lodging.

38. D: Although all of the answer choices contain subjective words, choice D is the correct answer because it is the only phrase that comes from a sentence expressing the author's opinion about Alaska. Choice A refers to Yosemite's Inspiration Point, not Alaska. Choice B refers to the long stretch of land from Omaha, Nebraska, to Portland, Oregon. Choice C refers to the size of Alaska rather than its good or bad qualities.

39. C: because paragraph 12 says that the totem pole represents the family tree (which refers to lineage) and also that the pole shows great events of the family. Choice A is incorrect because paragraph 12 says that Fort Wrangel was only prosperous when it was a mining town. Choice B is also incorrect because the decline of Fort Wrangel is related to the lack of excitement for mining rather than the presence of the totem poles. Choice D is incorrect because the totem poles represent the family of the Indians, not the more recent settlers.

40. D: Although all of the answer choices show a distance, choice D is the only correct answer because it is the only answer choice that refers to Alaska's size. Choice A is incorrect because 1,500 miles refers to the distance from Portland, Maine, to Omaha, Nebraska. Choice B is incorrect because 1,700 refers to the distance from Omaha to Portland, Oregon. Choice C is incorrect because it refers to the number of miles that the western edge of Alaska is west of San Francisco, California. However, this number of miles does not tell the readers anything about Alaska's size, only the location of its west coast.

41. B: is the correct answer because the author talks about the travelers' journey from the continental United States to the territory of Alaska; therefore, the passage is showing the beginning of the journey, rather than the end, making choice A is incorrect. Choice C is incorrect because paragraph 7 indicates that the travelers have never been to Alaska and are experiencing the sights for the first time. Choice D is incorrect because the narrator describes Alaska in great detail; therefore, the reader can assume that the narrator has been to Alaska.

42. C: because both selections describe travels. The narrator of *Roughing It* experiences the travels himself while the narrator of *Sights and Scenes* has traveled to Alaska before and is describing it so tourists can know what to expect. Choice A is incorrect because the narrators don't focus on the time they spent with other travelers. The narrator of *Roughing It* talks about the woman he met for a small part of the passage, but he mostly focuses on the journey. The narrator of *Sights and Scenes* describes the travelers but does not talk about how they get along. Choice B is incorrect because only a small portion of *Sights and Scenes* focuses on the history of Alaska. The narrator of *Roughing*

It does not talk about the history of the Plains. Choice D is incorrect because the passages do not focus on natural wonders. *Sights and Scenes* talks about the geography of Alaska but does not describe any particular features. The narrator in *Roughing It* describes the Plains but also does not talk about outstanding features.

43. A: because both narrators are excited about their journey and destination. The reader can see this excitement from the level of detail that the narrators share and the positive outlook that both narrators portray. Though the narrator of *Roughing It* is irritated while he talks to the woman on the stagecoach, choice B is incorrect because the narrator of *Sights and Scenes* does not show any irritation. Similarly, choice C is incorrect because the narrator of *Sights and Scenes* is never bored, even though the narrator of *Roughing It* is bored during the boat ride to St. Jo's. Choice D is incorrect because only the narrator of *Sights and Scenes* has prior experience with the land he is describing.

44. D: because both passages provide a lot of details about the land. Choice A is incorrect because only *Roughing It* has dialogue; furthermore, it's not a large part of the passage. Choices B and C are also incorrect because they only appear in *Roughing It.*

Part B: Since both passages contain a lot of details, any sentence that contains a lot of detail is an acceptable example. Example from *Roughing It:* And so, when he offered me, in cold blood, the sublime position of private secretary under him, it appeared to me that the heavens and the earth passed away, and the firmament was rolled together as a scroll!

Example from *The Project Gutenberg:* The Alaskan voyage is like a continuous dream of pleasure, so placid and quiet are the waters of the landlocked sea and so exquisitely beautiful the environment.

45. B: because the passage says that if a car is chartered for ten days or more, the cost per day is $5.00 less than what is shown in the table. Therefore, since the cost per day for a hotel car, as shown in the table, is $50, the cost per day for a 15-day trip is $45. Choice A is incorrect because it represents the cost per day for a buffet car rented for ten or more days, not a hotel car. Choice C is incorrect because it shows the cost per day for less than ten days. Choice D is incorrect because it shows the cost of the hotel car for the entire trip rather than the cost per day.

46. C: is the correct answer because the tables show the different rate options that travelers have. Choice A is incorrect because the passage doesn't tell specific passengers how much they might owe; instead, it gives a price list. Choice B is incorrect because the passage doesn't say how much a first class ticket costs; however, it does say that passengers need a first class ticket in order to stay in chartered cars. Choice D is incorrect because there is no diagram of the cars; however, one is available on request.

47. D: because the cars are intended for groups of fifteen people or more, according to the final paragraph of the passage. Therefore, a private individual, who is traveling alone, would be the least likely to charter a sleeping car. The groups described in choices A, B, and C could contain fifteen or more people and might charter a sleeping car.

Sample Short Answer Response

The phrase "roughing it" usually means to live with fewer comforts than usual. For example, when people go camping, they usually rough it because they sleep on the ground, don't have electricity, and don't have bathrooms. In Roughing It, the narrator and his brother are leaving their regular life and moving to the Nevada Territory. Since the passage says that it's the Nevada Territory rather than the state of Nevada, the reader can assume that the story takes place in the past and that the land may not be as developed as it is today. The narrator also shows how he and his brother were roughing it in paragraph 8 when he describes how they had to leave all of their fine clothes like their "swallow-tail coats and white kid gloves" behind. This example shows that the narrator and his brother had to leave the comforts of home behind.

48. A: because the passage says that Alice is 'burning with curiosity.' This means that Alice feels an intense curiosity about the White Rabbit. The other three choices are incorrect because they are referring to temperature or fire rather than the intensity of Alice's curiosity.

49. B: because Alice is feeling bored with sitting by her sister and doing nothing, she feels eager to follow the White Rabbit once he appears. Although the first sentence of paragraph 1 says Alice is getting tired, the word 'tired' is not referring to sleepiness, which makes choice A incorrect. Choice C is incorrect because Alice only feels curious after she sees the White Rabbit. The setting, however, makes her feel bored and restless. Choice D is incorrect because Alice says she doesn't feel like reading because her sister's book does not have pictures.

50. D: because Alice says that she has no idea what the words mean but that she thinks they are nice, big words. Choice A is incorrect because, although latitude and longitude can help people find locations on a map, Alice does not know what the words mean. Even though Alice says the words because they're big and impressive, choice B is incorrect because Alice has no one to show off to; she's alone in the rabbit hole. Choice C is incorrect because Alice does not listen for an echo or comment on hearing one.

51. B: is correct because the words are capitalized to emphasize the absurdity of Alice's situation. Choice A is incorrect because this passage is a finished, published excerpt that has already been proofread. Choice C is incorrect because Alice's demeanor shows that she is not upset by falling; in fact, she's intrigued by her new situation. Choice D is incorrect because there is no one else in the rabbit hole that Alice could talk to.

52. A: because Alice examines the bottle and tries to determine if it is poison. Choices B, C, and D are incorrect because Alice is not showing extreme emotion. Instead, she looks at the bottle very analytically and thinks carefully about whether or not she should drink from it.

53. C: the correct answer because Alice is worried that she will continue shrinking and go "out altogether, like a candle." Choice A is incorrect because Alice has already determined that the bottle is not poison. Choice B is incorrect because Alice and the reader have already seen proof that the liquid is working because Alice is getting smaller. Although Alice uses a flame analogy to explain her fears about shrinking forever, choice D is incorrect because Alice is not actually worried about turning into a flame.

54. Part A: D: is the correct answer because details from paragraphs 6-10, such as the extraordinarily long rabbit hole and the cupboards on the walls, show that the story is going to be fantasy. Because it is clear from these details that the story will contain elements that are not real, choice C is incorrect. Although falling through a rabbit hole might seem like a dangerous situation, choice A is incorrect because the passage doesn't convey any sense of urgency or danger. Instead, Alice is experiencing a leisurely fall through the rabbit hole. Choice B is incorrect because Alice portrays curiosity rather than nervousness.

Part B: D: This is the best answer, because if give an example of something that is fantasy. There is no way to fall through the center of the earth.

55. B: because the key only opens a very small door that Alice can't fit through. Choice A is incorrect because the text says that Alice uses the key to open one of the doors. Choice C is incorrect because Alice doesn't start shrinking until paragraph 18, after she drinks the liquid. Choice D is incorrect because Alice has been in a strange, unknown setting for most of the passage, not just in this paragraph.

56. C: Although there are many unusual things about the rabbit, choice C is correct because the author uses capitalization to show the unusualness of the rabbit's watch. Choice A is incorrect because the text says that there is nothing very remarkable in the pink eyes. Choice B is also incorrect because the text says that Alice doesn't think it is that unusual to hear the rabbit speak. Choice D is incorrect because Alice might expect a rabbit to go into a rabbit hole.

57. B: because the narrator says that she and Ed decided to have breakfast at Café A. She also says that she has never seen a worse breakfast. Although she drinks a cup of English Breakfast tea, choice A is not correct because the tea is only one part of the breakfast. Choice C is not correct because they buy the peppermints after they eat the breakfast, or repast. Although the narrator says she pities the subjects of King Edward (the King of England) if they have to drink the awful tea frequently, "repast" isn't referring to the King because it is something that is eaten.

58. Part A: C: because the narrator says that she is taking a boat along the St. Lawrence and comments on the huge castles and small cottages that she sees along the way. Choice A is incorrect because the narrator announces at the beginning of paragraph 1 that she has left the United States. Although the narrator mentions the Rhine River in paragraph 2, she is not on the Rhine yet. She's planning on journeying down the Rhine at a later date and says that she'll be disappointed if it is not more entrancing than the St. Lawrence. Choice D is incorrect because, although the narrator and Ed joke at the image of children playing in the river, they don't actually see any children.

Part B: B: This is the best answer because it talks about them going down the river and looking at all of the houses.

59: A: is correct because the narrator comments in paragraph 3 that "the castles are too new, the homes do not show the caress of time..." Choice B is incorrect because she wishes that the cottages and castles were older and is displeased that they are not. Choice C is incorrect because, although the narrator mentions that the Thousand Islands have 1,642 islands, she does not express anger about it. Choice D is incorrect because the narrator does not actually see any children playing while she sails through the Thousand Islands, she only imagines them playing in the river.

60. C: Although the narrator traveled all over Montreal, the best answer is choice C, when she views the city from up high on Mount Royal. She says in paragraph 11 that she is able to learn Montreal fairly well after looking at the city and listening to Ed describe all the buildings. Choice A is incorrect because the narrator sails through the Thousand Islands before arriving in Montreal. Although the narrator does eat at Café A, which is in Montreal, choice B is incorrect because the café is only one building in the entire city. Choice D is incorrect because Madame K. gives the narrator a tour of Convent of the Ladies of the Sacred Heart, not Montreal.

How to Overcome Test Anxiety

Just the thought of taking a test is enough to make most people a little nervous. A test is an important event that can have a long-term impact on your future, so it's important to take it seriously and it's natural to feel anxious about performing well. But just because anxiety is normal, that doesn't mean that it's helpful in test taking, or that you should simply accept it as part of your life. Anxiety can have a variety of effects. These effects can be mild, like making you feel slightly nervous, or severe, like blocking your ability to focus or remember even a simple detail.

If you experience test anxiety—whether severe or mild—it's important to know how to beat it. To discover this, first you need to understand what causes test anxiety.

Causes of Test Anxiety

While we often think of anxiety as an uncontrollable emotional state, it can actually be caused by simple, practical things. One of the most common causes of test anxiety is that a person does not feel adequately prepared for their test. This feeling can be the result of many different issues such as poor study habits or lack of organization, but the most common culprit is time management. Starting to study too late, failing to organize your study time to cover all of the material, or being distracted while you study will mean that you're not well prepared for the test. This may lead to cramming the night before, which will cause you to be physically and mentally exhausted for the test. Poor time management also contributes to feelings of stress, fear, and hopelessness as you realize you are not well prepared but don't know what to do about it.

Other times, test anxiety is not related to your preparation for the test but comes from unresolved fear. This may be a past failure on a test, or poor performance on tests in general. It may come from comparing yourself to others who seem to be performing better or from the stress of living up to expectations. Anxiety may be driven by fears of the future—how failure on this test would affect your educational and career goals. These fears are often completely irrational, but they can still negatively impact your test performance.

Elements of Test Anxiety

As mentioned earlier, test anxiety is considered to be an emotional state, but it has physical and mental components as well. Sometimes you may not even realize that you are suffering from test anxiety until you notice the physical symptoms. These can include trembling hands, rapid heartbeat, sweating, nausea, and tense muscles. Extreme anxiety may lead to fainting or vomiting. Obviously, any of these symptoms can have a negative impact on testing. It is important to recognize them as soon as they begin to occur so that you can address the problem before it damages your performance.

The mental components of test anxiety include trouble focusing and inability to remember learned information. During a test, your mind is on high alert, which can help you recall information and stay focused for an extended period of time. However, anxiety interferes with your mind's natural processes, causing you to blank out, even on the questions you know well. The strain of testing during anxiety makes it difficult to stay focused, especially on a test that may take several hours. Extreme anxiety can take a huge mental toll, making it difficult not only to recall test information but even to understand the test questions or pull your thoughts together.

Effects of Test Anxiety

Test anxiety is like a disease—if left untreated, it will get progressively worse. Anxiety leads to poor performance, and this reinforces the feelings of fear and failure, which in turn lead to poor performances on subsequent tests. It can grow from a mild nervousness to a crippling condition. If allowed to progress, test anxiety can have a big impact on your schooling, and consequently on your future.

Test anxiety can spread to other parts of your life. Anxiety on tests can become anxiety in any stressful situation, and blanking on a test can turn into panicking in a job situation. But fortunately, you don't have to let anxiety rule your testing and determine your grades. There are a number of relatively simple steps you can take to move past anxiety and function normally on a test and in the rest of life.

Physical Steps for Beating Test Anxiety

While test anxiety is a serious problem, the good news is that it can be overcome. It doesn't have to control your ability to think and remember information. While it may take time, you can begin taking steps today to beat anxiety.

Just as your first hint that you may be struggling with anxiety comes from the physical symptoms, the first step to treating it is also physical. Rest is crucial for having a clear, strong mind. If you are tired, it is much easier to give in to anxiety. But if you establish good sleep habits, your body and mind will be ready to perform optimally, without the strain of exhaustion. Additionally, sleeping well helps you to retain information better, so you're more likely to recall the answers when you see the test questions.

Getting good sleep means more than going to bed on time. It's important to allow your brain time to relax. Take study breaks from time to time so it doesn't get overworked, and don't study right before bed. Take time to rest your mind before trying to rest your body, or you may find it difficult to fall asleep.

Along with sleep, other aspects of physical health are important in preparing for a test. Good nutrition is vital for good brain function. Sugary foods and drinks may give a burst of energy but this burst is followed by a crash, both physically and emotionally. Instead, fuel your body with protein and vitamin-rich foods.

Also, drink plenty of water. Dehydration can lead to headaches and exhaustion, especially if your brain is already under stress from the rigors of the test. Particularly if your test is a long one, drink water during the breaks. And if possible, take an energy-boosting snack to eat between sections.

Along with sleep and diet, a third important part of physical health is exercise. Maintaining a steady workout schedule is helpful, but even taking 5-minute study breaks to walk can help get your blood pumping faster and clear your head. Exercise also releases endorphins, which contribute to a positive feeling and can help combat test anxiety.

When you nurture your physical health, you are also contributing to your mental health. If your body is healthy, your mind is much more likely to be healthy as well. So take time to rest, nourish your body with healthy food and water, and get moving as much as possible. Taking these physical steps will make you stronger and more able to take the mental steps necessary to overcome test anxiety.

Mental Steps for Beating Test Anxiety

Working on the mental side of test anxiety can be more challenging, but as with the physical side, there are clear steps you can take to overcome it. As mentioned earlier, test anxiety often stems from lack of preparation, so the obvious solution is to prepare for the test. Effective studying may be the most important weapon you have for beating test anxiety, but you can and should employ several other mental tools to combat fear.

First, boost your confidence by reminding yourself of past success—tests or projects that you aced. If you're putting as much effort into preparing for this test as you did for those, there's no reason you should expect to fail here. Work hard to prepare; then trust your preparation.

Second, surround yourself with encouraging people. It can be helpful to find a study group, but be sure that the people you're around will encourage a positive attitude. If you spend time with others who are anxious or cynical, this will only contribute to your own anxiety. Look for others who are motivated to study hard from a desire to succeed, not from a fear of failure.

Third, reward yourself. A test is physically and mentally tiring, even without anxiety, and it can be helpful to have something to look forward to. Plan an activity following the test, regardless of the outcome, such as going to a movie or getting ice cream.

When you are taking the test, if you find yourself beginning to feel anxious, remind yourself that you know the material. Visualize successfully completing the test. Then take a few deep, relaxing breaths and return to it. Work through the questions carefully but with confidence, knowing that you are capable of succeeding.

Developing a healthy mental approach to test taking will also aid in other areas of life. Test anxiety affects more than just the actual test—it can be damaging to your mental health and even contribute to depression. It's important to beat test anxiety before it becomes a problem for more than testing.

Study Strategy

Being prepared for the test is necessary to combat anxiety, but what does being prepared look like? You may study for hours on end and still not feel prepared. What you need is a strategy for test prep. The next few pages outline our recommended steps to help you plan out and conquer the challenge of preparation.

Step 1: Scope Out the Test

Learn everything you can about the format (multiple choice, essay, etc.) and what will be on the test. Gather any study materials, course outlines, or sample exams that may be available. Not only will this help you to prepare, but knowing what to expect can help to alleviate test anxiety.

Step 2: Map Out the Material

Look through the textbook or study guide and make note of how many chapters or sections it has. Then divide these over the time you have. For example, if a book has 15 chapters and you have five days to study, you need to cover three chapters each day. Even better, if you have the time, leave an extra day at the end for overall review after you have gone through the material in depth.

If time is limited, you may need to prioritize the material. Look through it and make note of which sections you think you already have a good grasp on, and which need review. While you are studying, skim quickly through the familiar sections and take more time on the challenging parts.

Write out your plan so you don't get lost as you go. Having a written plan also helps you feel more in control of the study, so anxiety is less likely to arise from feeling overwhelmed at the amount to cover.

Step 3: Gather Your Tools

Decide what study method works best for you. Do you prefer to highlight in the book as you study and then go back over the highlighted portions? Or do you type out notes of the important information? Or is it helpful to make flashcards that you can carry with you? Assemble the pens, index cards, highlighters, post-it notes, and any other materials you may need so you won't be distracted by getting up to find things while you study.

If you're having a hard time retaining the information or organizing your notes, experiment with different methods. For example, try color-coding by subject with colored pens, highlighters, or post-it notes. If you learn better by hearing, try recording yourself reading your notes so you can listen while in the car, working out, or simply sitting at your desk. Ask a friend to quiz you from your flashcards, or try teaching someone the material to solidify it in your mind.

Step 4: Create Your Environment

It's important to avoid distractions while you study. This includes both the obvious distractions like visitors and the subtle distractions like an uncomfortable chair (or a too-comfortable couch that makes you want to fall asleep). Set up the best study environment possible: good lighting and a comfortable work area. If background music helps you focus, you may want to turn it on, but otherwise keep the room quiet. If you are using a computer to take notes, be sure you don't have any other windows open, especially applications like social media, games, or anything else that could distract you. Silence your phone and turn off notifications. Be sure to keep water close by so you stay hydrated while you study (but avoid unhealthy drinks and snacks).

Also, take into account the best time of day to study. Are you freshest first thing in the morning? Try to set aside some time then to work through the material. Is your mind clearer in the afternoon or evening? Schedule your study session then. Another method is to study at the same time of day that you will take the test, so that your brain gets used to working on the material at that time and will be ready to focus at test time.

Step 5: Study!

Once you have done all the study preparation, it's time to settle into the actual studying. Sit down, take a few moments to settle your mind so you can focus, and begin to follow your study plan. Don't give in to distractions or let yourself procrastinate. This is your time to prepare so you'll be ready to fearlessly approach the test. Make the most of the time and stay focused.

Of course, you don't want to burn out. If you study too long you may find that you're not retaining the information very well. Take regular study breaks. For example, taking five minutes out of every hour to walk briskly, breathing deeply and swinging your arms, can help your mind stay fresh.

As you get to the end of each chapter or section, it's a good idea to do a quick review. Remind yourself of what you learned and work on any difficult parts. When you feel that you've mastered the material, move on to the next part. At the end of your study session, briefly skim through your notes again.

But while review is helpful, cramming last minute is NOT. If at all possible, work ahead so that you won't need to fit all your study into the last day. Cramming overloads your brain with more information than it can process and retain, and your tired mind may struggle to recall even previously learned information when it is overwhelmed with last-minute study. Also, the urgent nature of cramming and the stress placed on your brain contribute to anxiety. You'll be more likely to go to the test feeling unprepared and having trouble thinking clearly.

So don't cram, and don't stay up late before the test, even just to review your notes at a leisurely pace. Your brain needs rest more than it needs to go over the information again. In fact, plan to finish your studies by noon or early afternoon the day before the test. Give your brain the rest of the day to relax or focus on other things, and get a good night's sleep. Then you will be fresh for the test and better able to recall what you've studied.

Step 6: Take a Practice Test

Many courses offer sample tests, either online or in the study materials. This is an excellent resource to check whether you have mastered the material, as well as to prepare for the test format and environment.

Check the test format ahead of time: the number of questions, the type (multiple choice, free response, etc.), and the time limit. Then create a plan for working through them. For example, if you have 30 minutes to take a 60-question test, your limit is 30 seconds per question. Spend less time on the questions you know well so that you can take more time on the difficult ones.

If you have time to take several practice tests, take the first one open book, with no time limit. Work through the questions at your own pace and make sure you fully understand them. Gradually work up to taking a test under test conditions: sit at a desk with all study materials put away and set a timer. Pace yourself to make sure you finish the test with time to spare and go back to check your answers if you have time.

After each test, check your answers. On the questions you missed, be sure you understand why you missed them. Did you misread the question (tests can use tricky wording)? Did you forget the information? Or was it something you hadn't learned? Go back and study any shaky areas that the practice tests reveal.

Taking these tests not only helps with your grade, but also aids in combating test anxiety. If you're already used to the test conditions, you're less likely to worry about it, and working through tests until you're scoring well gives you a confidence boost. Go through the practice tests until you feel comfortable, and then you can go into the test knowing that you're ready for it.

Test Tips

On test day, you should be confident, knowing that you've prepared well and are ready to answer the questions. But aside from preparation, there are several test day strategies you can employ to maximize your performance.

First, as stated before, get a good night's sleep the night before the test (and for several nights before that, if possible). Go into the test with a fresh, alert mind rather than staying up late to study.

Try not to change too much about your normal routine on the day of the test. It's important to eat a nutritious breakfast, but if you normally don't eat breakfast at all, consider eating just a protein bar. If you're a coffee drinker, go ahead and have your normal coffee. Just make sure you time it so that the caffeine doesn't wear off right in the middle of your test. Avoid sugary beverages, and drink enough water to stay hydrated but not so much that you need a restroom break 10 minutes into the test. If your test isn't first thing in the morning, consider going for a walk or doing a light workout before the test to get your blood flowing.

Allow yourself enough time to get ready, and leave for the test with plenty of time to spare so you won't have the anxiety of scrambling to arrive in time. Another reason to be early is to select a good seat. It's helpful to sit away from doors and windows, which can be distracting. Find a good seat, get out your supplies, and settle your mind before the test begins.

When the test begins, start by going over the instructions carefully, even if you already know what to expect. Make sure you avoid any careless mistakes by following the directions.

Then begin working through the questions, pacing yourself as you've practiced. If you're not sure on an answer, don't spend too much time on it, and don't let it shake your confidence. Either skip it and come back later, or eliminate as many wrong answers as possible and guess among the remaining ones. Don't dwell on these questions as you continue—put them out of your mind and focus on what lies ahead.

Be sure to read all of the answer choices, even if you're sure the first one is the right answer. Sometimes you'll find a better one if you keep reading. But don't second-guess yourself if you do immediately know the answer. Your gut instinct is usually right. Don't let test anxiety rob you of the information you know.

If you have time at the end of the test (and if the test format allows), go back and review your answers. Be cautious about changing any, since your first instinct tends to be correct, but make sure you didn't misread any of the questions or accidentally mark the wrong answer choice. Look over any you skipped and make an educated guess.

At the end, leave the test feeling confident. You've done your best, so don't waste time worrying about your performance or wishing you could change anything. Instead, celebrate the successful completion of this test. And finally, use this test to learn how to deal with anxiety even better next time.

Review Video: Test Anxiety
Visit mometrix.com/academy and enter code: 100340

Important Qualification

Not all anxiety is created equal. If your test anxiety is causing major issues in your life beyond the classroom or testing center, or if you are experiencing troubling physical symptoms related to your anxiety, it may be a sign of a serious physiological or psychological condition. If this sounds like your situation, we strongly encourage you to seek professional help.

Thank You

We at Mometrix would like to extend our heartfelt thanks to you, our friend and patron, for allowing us to play a part in your journey. It is a privilege to serve people from all walks of life who are unified in their commitment to building the best future they can for themselves.

The preparation you devote to these important testing milestones may be the most valuable educational opportunity you have for making a real difference in your life. We encourage you to put your heart into it—that feeling of succeeding, overcoming, and yes, conquering will be well worth the hours you've invested.

We want to hear your story, your struggles and your successes, and if you see any opportunities for us to improve our materials so we can help others even more effectively in the future, please share that with us as well. **The team at Mometrix would be absolutely thrilled to hear from you!** So please, send us an email (support@mometrix.com) and let's stay in touch.

If you'd like some additional help, check out these other resources we offer for your exam:
http://MometrixFlashcards.com/CCSS

Online Resources

Due to our efforts to try to keep this book to a manageable length, we've created a link that will give you access to all of your online resources:

mometrix.com/resources719/ccg12ela

It's Your Moment, Let's Celebrate It!

Share your story @mometrixtestpreparation